A Sunshine in the Shady Place

A LITTLE MERMAN.

(See page 96.)

A

...NE IN THE SHADY PLACE

...

HOULSTON ...

PATERNOSTER SQUARE

MDCCC...

A

SUNSHINE IN THE SHADY PLACE.

BY

EDITH MILNER,

AUTHOR OF "FITFUL GLEAMS FROM FANCY LAND," "D'EYNCOURT
MANOR," "THE LILY OF LUMLEY," ETC.

"Her angel's face,
As the great eye of heaven, shynèd bright,
And made a sunshine in the shady place;
Did never mortall eye behold such heavenly grace."
                    SPENSER'S *Faerie Queene, Canto III.*
                            Una and the Lion.

LONDON

HOULSTON AND SONS,

PATERNOSTER SQUARE.

MDCCCLXXVI.

UNWIN BROTHERS, THE GRESHAM PRESS, CHILWORTH AND LONDON.

Dedication

TO MY NEPHEW, GUY FAIRFAX.

———

" PERCHANCE as finding *here* some image of thyself,"
And in the years which now far distant seem,
But which in truth will glide on like a dream,
Teeming, I trust, with boyhood's healthy joy,
Cricket and manly sports, with youth's alloy
The needful work, to harden the pure gold,
Which else would bend if play were the tale told
Of thy young life ;—when finished years shall bring
The longed-for manhood, and joy-bells shall ring
To tell of little lives begun, like thine
A few short years ago, a bright sunshine
To make, as thou hast made, this tale grown old
May find fresh youth in pranks of youngsters bold,
Who laugh well-pleased to find that thou hast done
The selfsame tricks, the selfsame course hast run.

EDITH MILNER.

Nun-Appleton.

CONTENTS.

———◆———

A Sunshine in the Shady Place.

CHAPTER I.

CHANGES.

A STREET in London—a bitterly cold day in January. A cab draws up with some difficulty at the door of a house in a well-known part of the town. A lady gets out with such a bright pleasant face that even now, though she looks sad and anxious, the cabman observes to a mate that "Yon face is better than sunshine." She pays him his just fare, giving neither more nor less than his due, and does it in such a manner that she satisfies one of a race which is usually hard to satisfy. The door of the house has meantime been opened quietly a man has lifted a small portmanteau and travelling-bag into the passage, and in another moment the door is closed as quietly as it had been opened. Although it is barely three o'clock, it is so dark that the gas is turned on everywhere, both out-of-doors and indoors. It is light enough by this means to see that a shadow

2

of some great evil is threatening the peace of that household. The servant looks sad; the new-comer can hardly restrain her tears after a whispered word with a nurse who comes forward to take her bag from her hand; even a little boy of five years old, who almost tumbles downstairs headlong in his eagerness to greet one who is evidently a friend, has tears in his bright eyes.

"It is so horrid, so quiet, so dull," he says, breathlessly, kissing Auntie, as he calls her, again and again. "Father does not look at me; and Mammy—ah!" he said, cutting himself short, "she says I am to call her Mother. It is a very nice name, but Mammy is comfortabler."

"More comfortable," suggests auntie, as she smiles and gives him her hand for him to lead her into mother's room.

"Mother is going away from us," the boy continues, as the pair go softly up the long staircase. "She does not want to go, but Jesus has called her, and the angels are waiting for her. Father says he is willing to let her go—I heard him say that—but she said she could not, could not leave him. She said nothing about leaving me, but I daresay she really is sorry about leaving me too. She is going to take poor little baby away with her. She has got your name, that baby has, but she is not like you; she cannot speak, and I do not think she can breathe."

The lady's tears, which had been near enough to her eyes ever since a telegram had summoned her to her only sister's deathbed, were flowing silently now, while Geoffrey told his artless story. But he must hush, and his aunt must compose herself, for they are at the door of mother's room.

The father, mother, and little babe are the only occupants of that room. The doctors have gone. "Nothing can save her," and so they will not weary her with useless experiments. Baby needs no nurse as she lies still and waxlike in unearthly beauty in the little cot out of which rosy Geoffrey tumbled when he outgrew it more than four years ago. Baby's fingers are folded round some pure white snowdrops, which are yet scarcely as fair as baby's face.

On the large bed, baby's mother, though almost as white as baby, still breathes, still struggles with the stern reaper called Death, who, as the poem says,—

> Reaps the bearded grain, . . .
> And the flowers that grow between.

The bearded grain means the aged people who have finished their earthly life, who are generally glad enough to bow their heads to the sickle; in other words, to die on earth in order to live in heaven. The flowers that death claims too often for the happiness of those who have to live without them are the young fathers and mothers, the brothers and sisters, who, when they are gathered by death, leave such an empty place in the homes which they have brightened. Death sometimes takes buds, too, like the little baby who had died that morning as quietly and as happily as a very old person might die. The clergyman had given it to God first, he

2 *

had poured water on its little face, and signed on the white brow the sign of the cross which it would never have to bear on earth. Now baby is wearing a crown which has been won for her, while her poor mother is praying to stay a little longer here below.

Certainly life has been no vale of tears for her, she has been more blessed than most mortals, her first and last trial assails her now. She could have let the baby go, she thinks, much as she had wished for a little daughter, for her husband's sake even more than for her own, but she could not bow to God's whole decree. Gentle and holy as she had always been, this rebellion against Providence at the last made the heavy trial almost unbearable. In vain the clergyman urged resignation, in vain her husband practised it, she seemed like one possessed.

When Eleanor entered the room she had been quiet for some time from sheer exhaustion, but the sight of her sister roused her, and her sad plaintive murmurs began again.

Eleanor quietly kissed her on the lips and so silenced her, then she took her hand, knelt down, and prayed, in language that the little boy, who instinctively knelt beside her, understood, that God would take away the evil spirit, and give her the peace which passeth understanding before He took her to Himself.

Geoffrey said afterwards, " She prayed like I pray— she asked God for what she wanted and it seemed to come."

Before Eleanor had finished, the impatient restless

look gave place to the sweet bright one which had been her usual expression, the dying woman smiled again, and held out her disengaged hand to her husband. "Darling,", she said, "forgive me." During the seven happy years of their married life there had never been any need on either side to ask forgiveness.

"Mother is good now," whispered Geoffrey; "perhaps she will remember me too."

And, with her husband's hand in hers, she did indeed seem to remember something. "My child. Eleanor, you will be his mother."

And then the little fellow threw himself into her arms.

"Mother, when I was little I used to call you mammy. I will call her *amie*—that is French for friend, and it is like mammy; mother is the best friend, and she will be next best."

Then his next best friend took him away, and the husband and wife were alone again. But Eleanor left behind her the peace which might be called her attendant spirit, and her sister blessed her with almost her last breath. Her actual last word was for her husband, and when next her little boy saw her, for the last time, her spirit had joined her baby's spirit, her face was smiling as calmly now as baby's face.

Geoffrey did not cry, and his aunt was at first inclined to think that he showed a want of feeling; afterwards she learned to understand him better.

Geoffrey was a thorough boy, hitherto he had never known a sorrow, his little life had been full of joy; his parents indulged him without spoiling him, and when this first trouble came he was too young to realise what he had lost. Like all children, he was fond of change; he was going with his aunt to uncle Arthur's beautiful house in the country, while father went to Italy to carve a lovely white marble mother and baby-sister, and his little mind could not look on any further. Perhaps he thought dimly that the marble mother might take the place of his mother whom God wanted for Himself; anyhow, mother had given him to auntie, and he was going to call her *amie*, and he did not like being unhappy, it was so uncomfortable, so that he was going to be a good boy, and try to make them all happy, and be as happy as possible himself.

We must now give a little account of aunt Eleanor and of Geoffrey's father and mother.

Eleanor and Marion Norman had lost their parents before they could realise the loss, and they had been brought up at the old family place, Normanhurst, by a childless uncle and aunt. They had one brother called Arthur, who was the heir to the old place; and the kind uncle and aunt never let them feel the want of parents.

Mrs. Norman had a nephew whom she loved as dearly as she loved her children, for so she liked to call the little Normans, and as they grew up, and Geoffrey Gordon found out that Marion Norman was dearer to him than even her sister Eleanor, dearly as he loved them both, Mr. and Mrs. Norman gladly consented to their marriage.

Geoffrey had chosen art for a profession, from natural inclination, he had a comfortable fortune of his own; and at the time when we first make his acquaintance he was already known to fame both for his paintings and for his statues.

Mr. and Mrs. Norman lived to see their great-nephew christened, they had the happiness of witnessing the bliss of these two people who were so dear to them, and they died within a few weeks of each other, Mrs. Norman from the results of a neglected cold which ended in acute bronchitis, and Mr. Norman because he could not live without his wife.

Arthur Norman succeeded to the grand old place, and to all the wealth which Mr. Norman left him, upon condition that a home was secured at Normanhurst for Eleanor as long as she should remain unmarried.

Young Mr. Norman gladly consented to this arrangement, being very fond of his sister. A sad trouble, however, fell upon him shortly after he took possession of the property. He was going to be married to a young lady to whom he had been deeply attached since his boyhood; the week before his marriage he found out that she did not really care for him, and he took upon himself the blame of breaking off the engagement to save her. She had not deceived him intentionally, she liked him very much, it was only when she realised that she was going to marry him that she found out that she liked her own home, her own father and mother, and brothers and sisters better than she liked poor Arthur.

In short, she did not love him, and she was quite right to let him know the true state of the case before it was too late. She had married since a poor clergyman, for whose sake she cheerfully left her happy, comfortable home, and all her dear ones, and she was now making his little parsonage-house a regular sun-trap.

It was very hard upon Arthur, and he had not borne it very well. He behaved most honourably and kindly in the first instance, but when all was over he settled down at Normanhurst, a gloomy disappointed man. He did his duty by his tenantry, his cottages were models for every landlord, his place was in the most perfect order; but he shunned society, he never entertained his neighbours, and he did not respond when his bright sunny-natured sister tried to rouse him from his gloomy silent reserve. She was certainly "a sunshine in the shady place," but her lion was a very unapproachable lion. One of our greatest poets tells a beautiful story about a lady called Una, who by her goodness and her purity overcame a great many dangers; amongst others, she conquered the savage nature of a lion, who became her champion. The story is a long one, too long to tell here, and it is an allegory, which is a story containing a meaning inside a meaning. One meaning is very apparent. This Una conquered the lion, and all the other dangers through which she passed, by her virtues, which are often better weapons than swords and spears wielded by strong arms.

Now Arthur's moody spirit was the lion which Eleanor had set herself to subdue, and it was her influence which helped him to do his duty, which had he been left to himself he might have neglected, so fast was he bound by the chains of this sorrow to which he had given way.

Eleanor hoped, by making his home bright by her unvarying cheerfulness, that he might in time rouse himself and enjoy the many good things which he possessed, and thus cease to mourn so hopelessly for the one thing which had been denied him. He might learn at last that it was as much for his good that this trouble had been sent as were all the actual good things that he did possess.

He came up to London when he heard of his sister's death, and Eleanor could not help hoping that the sight of Mr. Gordon's patience might impress her brother. At present it seemed only to surprise him, and he was evidently inclined to attribute it to want of really deep feeling. Eleanor knew well how far this was from being the case, and she knew that Arthur would recognise the fact in time, and therefore made no comment, but let the seed sow itself, and trusted to time to develop it into a useful plant. Mr. Gordon is going to Italy to study art. He does not wish to forget, he knows he never can forget; but he is one who must occupy himself, and he feels that a spring in England without his darling wife would be more than even he, with all his resignation, would be able to bear.

His boy is to go to Normanhurst with Arthur and Eleanor, and with Geoffrey's first experience of country life our story will next have to do.

•

CHAPTER II.

PROGRESS.

GEOFFREY had never been in the country except for a few days at a time. His father had no country place, and though he had plenty of kind friends he had no relations.

Mr. and Mrs. Gordon were very much devoted to their only child, for such he was until baby came to take the mother away altogether. But they did not expect every one to enter into their feelings, and so they never took him with them when they visited their friends unless they were really warmly pressed to do so. Mr. Gordon was always so busy that he could not spare time for long visits; and when he and his wife went on their summer sketching tour Geoffrey had hitherto been too young to accompany them, either for their comfort or for his own enjoyment. He had never been at Norman-hurst since his christening, and now he was going to live there, for perhaps a year. A year! what might not a year bring forth? Certainly knickerbockers, perhaps manhood. The former were a certainty, because Amie had taken him to the shop he always called *Swares well*, to have him measured for those most desirable garments.

As to the manhood, he asked his father one morning when he was shaving whether it hurt? His father replied with perfect veracity, "Sometimes, especially on a cold morning."

Geoffrey looked earnestly at his own soft rosy face, and felt sorrowfully that it would indeed be superfluous pain in his case. Then he looked at his hair, which curled all over his head in little close rings, which mother used to put her fingers through so fondly, he remembered. No, he would not shave them off, because she had so often played with them and kissed them; and his eyes filled with tears when he remembered she could never do it again. But the shaving subject was very absorbing, and, with the tears still in his eyes, he began to look himself well over. His bare legs finally caught his attention; they would shave, anyhow, quite as well as father's face. He felt both, and satisfied himself that the legs were at least as rough, if not rougher, than the face. Of the two the former were the most hairy, for Mr. Gordon did not wear either beard or whiskers. Geoffrey began to wonder if shaving his legs would turn him into a man. It was the day before the little party was to break up. Father was going straight to Italy the very next day, and uncle Arthur and aunt Eleanor were going to take him to Normanhurst.

Uncle Arthur wore a beard and did not shave; besides, Geoffrey would not have used his razors for the world. They might turn him into a man like his uncle, a man who neither laughed nor smiled, and who very seldom spoke, except indeed to answer shortly when he was spoken to. No; poor uncle Arthur! Geoffrey pitied him sincerely. He did not seem to know how to enjoy life, and Geoffrey did know how, so thoroughly; it would be a pity to lose the power of enjoyment by becoming a man like him in a minute by using uncle Arthur's razors.

At last father's room was deserted for a time. The servants' dinner-bell rang, the valet had just been sorting the dressing things, they were all open on the table. The squeeze bottle, as Geoffrey called the modern contrivance for shaving-soap, was quite handy. The razors and strop were also on the table.

The looking-glass was quite at his service, with no father reflected in it. But it would be no use to him, he must look at his legs, and he very much feared he should have to sit on the floor to perform the operation in the most undignified manner; but, after all, what did it matter, if he rose from that floor a man?

The shaving-soap was very unmanageable; it spluttered all over his legs like lumps of butter—he had forgotten the hot water. Well, perhaps he could make it right with the strop. So he proceeded to try and spread it butter-wise, as if his legs had been bread. It was not a very successful operation so far. There was no symptom of lather, but, after all, the use of the razor was the point at which he was aiming. At this moment his aunt, who had been looking for him ever since the servants' dinner-bell had rung, entered the dressing-room. She stood quite still for a minute, gazing with terror on the open razor in the boy's hand.

"Geoffrey !"—she spoke quite gently and calmly— "put that down."

"Oh, Amie dear," he said, with the prettiest stress on the last syllable, "you have just come in time to see whether shaving my legs will change me into a man without the trouble of growing up. I cannot make the soap lather. I believe father uses hot water, and I cannot find the shaving-brush ; but I should think the razor is the most important thing."

By this time his aunt was sitting on the floor beside him, examining his little mottled legs, curiously smeared with soap, very anxiously.

"I have not begun to shave them with the razor," he said, thinking she was quite entering into the experiment.

"Now, Geoffrey dear," she said, "give me the razor."

"Do you think it will be the same if you do it?" he said, doubtfully, but handing her the razor, for he was a very obedient little boy.

"Now, Geoffrey, you must promise me something. You might have done yourself great harm, for razors are very sharp. You might have cut a vein and bled to death. Nothing will make you a man but time and patience. Your dear mother asked me to take care of you, but I cannot do this if you do not help me by taking care of yourself."

"*What* a pity you came in, Amie. I do much worse things than this I am sure."

This assertion was not consoling, but Eleanor before the interview was over secured a promise that he would never touch knives or razors, or anything that could cut.

"I wish you had been cross," he said, with a great sigh.

"Why?" she asked, very naturally.

"Because then I don't think I should have obeyed you, but you ask me to do things just as mother did, and I think it is rather a mean thing to do."

"Well, I don't mind being mean in that way," was the laughing answer, "if you will always do what I ask you."

His aunt had washed off the soap while she was talking, making for a short delightful moment the manly lather Geoffrey had failed to produce, and she had put everything tidy before the valet returned.

"It is lucky for you Miss Norman came," said Geoffrey; "I had been making a nice mess."

"Not the first time either, sir," said the valet, quite good-naturedly. "Thank you, ma'am," he added, respectfully, "it is just what Mrs. Gordon would have done."

And at the mention of his mother Geoffrey's laughing eyes filled with tears, and he trotted silently out of the room after his aunt.

Even Arthur laughed at Eleanor's account of the scene, and Mr. Gordon made a spirited little sketch of the boy and his aunt, with the proverb written below,—

"Great cry, little wool, as the shepherd said when he shaved the pig."

Geoffrey came in at this moment in his new suit, conscious that he had made a real step towards at least boyhood.

"You will never call me a child again, will you?" he said, as he rubbed his face against his father's.

It was too much for Mr. Gordon. He had been so brave ever since the doctors had said no human power could save his wife, but now that he was going to part with their child, seeing him thus for the first time in boy's clothes, being asked to recognise his boyhood, and Marion not beside him to laugh and to sigh, he felt as if he could not bear it.

How Marion would have laughed at the boy's assumption of manliness! How she would have sighed, but only in make-believe, at his actual boyishness.

Mr. Gordon left the room, and Geoffrey proved himself his mother's own son then; for he followed his father and, nestling into his arms as if he had been a daughter, instead of a boy aiming at manhood, he kissed him and whispered about all the comforting things his Amie had told him, until Mr. Gordon recovered his composure, and father and son went back to spend the last evening with Arthur and Eleanor.

After Geoffrey had gone to bed they talked much of his future. The elder Geoffrey knew that his wife and her sister agreed on the subject of education, and he had trusted Marion entirely on that subject. Now he gave up the charge of his boy with equal unreserve to the aunt; and after Arthur left the room the two who had so thoroughly appreciated her talked of Marion as if she were still with them. She was in truth only "gone before," not lost to them, and they liked best to say "she is," not "she was."

Before Mr. Gordon parted with his son he gave him a most lovely miniature of his mother, and the boy made his aunt hang it round his neck, saying, "She used to carry me, now I carry her."

And the first night that he said his prayers after he received the miniature he held it in his hands, and looked at the fair sweet face all the time.

His aunt remonstrated at first—he was kneeling at her knee—and she feared the contemplation of the face might distract his attention, or, still worse, engender a sort of superstition which might end in a kind of intercessory worship; that is, that he might pray through the picture. But his simple answer reproved her for her want of faith in the child's rightmindedness.

"I used to look at her when I said my prayers, and it always made me mind. When I had only your knee, Amie, it did not do nearly so well, and your face never looks quite so good as hers does. You are very nice, and you help me not to miss her much, but I do want her sometimes. Now I have got her face for my prayers I can mind them very nicely, and I can remember what she used to make me say. Her lips in the picture seem to say the words just as they did when she was alive."

Did his aunt still think him wanting in deep feeling? He puzzled her, for he parted with his father so cheerfully on the following morning that she thought he could not know what a long parting was before him. Perhaps he did not realise what time meant. He knew a year contained twelve months, that each month contained four weeks and a spare day or two, and that each week was made up of seven days, so that he could not see his father again for at least three hundred and sixty-five days ; but then he had such untasted joys to look forward to, and each joy having been partaken of would have to be remembered for father's benefit, so that he really did not feel very unhappy. He must part with his father in order to attain these untasted joys, and then detail them to father. He did not say all this, or even think that he thought it, but it was all arranged somewhere in his little busy head, and his aunt found it all out by degrees. Those two found each other out by signs and deeds and not by words, and thus got so closely linked together that a more perfect understanding and friendship existed between them than is often found on earth.

But now the three oddly assorted people are in the train. Uncle Arthur reads his paper pertinaciously and morosely ; aunt Eleanor responds pleasantly to all Geoffrey's remarks, though she has got a very amusing book, which she read almost by ejaculations, so incessant were Geoffrey's observations. These, written down, would always have required notes of admiration. "What a pace we are going, Amie ! Goodness me, what a jump ! Oh, look !" And so on for an hour or two, until it struck him that it was not quite good manners to leave uncle Arthur so completely out of the conversation, and therefore, leaving his seat opposite his aunt, he squeezed himself into a corner left vacant by his uncle's possessions, which were arranged opposite to him. Arthur never looked up, not even when he turned the paper over, and Geoffrey did not quite know how to break the silence.

3

Eleanor was enjoying her book thoroughly, and did not waste time by wondering what was occupying her nephew's attention. He was completely taken up with trying to catch his uncle's eye, when a sudden jolt upset his very precarious balance on the edge of the seat. He was thrown forward on his uncle's knee, his head went right through the intervening paper, and his eyes were brought in as close contact as noses would permit with Arthur's eyes.

The concussion caused both pairs of eyes to overflow, and Geoffrey was so delighted to find that his uncle seemed to be crying as involuntarily as himself, that he dried his own eyes with his coat-sleeve in order to feast them undimmed on the unexpected sight.

"Uncle Arthur is crying because my nose knocked his," he exclaimed as soon as he could speak. The paper was still round his neck, one hand firmly grasped his uncle's beard, which he had seized to steady himself when he first fell forwards, and he had shaken himself down quite comfortably on the unoffered seat his uncle's knees made for him. It was a strange way of storming a heart, but it answered completely ; a friendship began from that moment, which time ripened slowly but surely. As for aunt Eleanor she laughed till she cried ; and Arthur made himself quite pleasant to both his companions for the rest of the journey.

CHAPTER III.

THE NEW HOME.

THE short winter day was drawing to a close. The little party had left London in a thick fog, but for some days the frost, which had been very severe, had shown symptoms of giving way. January had turned into February, a miracle of monthly occurrence which puzzled and rather worried Geoffrey. He thought one name would have done for the whole year, or at most two, one for the winter and one for the summer, and he would have liked an easy name. The present month was the shortest, and it certainly had the hardest name—which Geoffrey, after much hesitation, generally pronounced Feb*ua*wy.

And now the train is stopping at a small station. It has not stopped before at so insignificant a place, and heads appear at more than one first-class carriage, and cross voices ask the meaning of the stoppage. "It is all right," answer the station-master and porter as they bustle about, but the passengers seem still to think it is all wrong.

Geoffrey does not restore their equanimity, though one or two who are more good-natured than the others cannot help laughing when he volunteers to say,—

3 *

"There is no accident. The train is only stopping for me, and uncle, and aunt."

The sun was setting brightly, the air was clear and crisp, and the little cockney, as his aunt called her town-bred nephew, was wondering at all the country sights and sounds.

He was particularly delighted with the vernacular, or accent with which the country people spoke, though he could not understand all they said.

Eleanor seemed quite at home with every one, Arthur occupied himself with the luggage, and only nodded silently in answer to the respectful greetings of the handful of farmers who are generally to be seen, especially on Saturdays, at small stations like Hurst.

"Please, 'm, may yon be Miss Marion's little one," asked a motherly-looking woman, with tears in her bright kind eyes.

"Yes, Mary," was the answer, "the only one, and I have got the sole charge of it. I feel rather like that cross old hen of yours who never brought up any chickens, but who once did hatch a whole brood of ducklings. How she did scold when they took to the water!"

"You old or cross, Miss Norman—the bonniest and the sweetest young lady, except her we have lost, that the sun ever shone on!"

Eleanor smiled as she shook her head and gave Geoffrey her hand, having showed him how to touch his hat in answer to country greetings, like uncle Arthur. He did it, as he did everything, with the prettiest grace

in the world, and more than one of those stalwart
farmers complained of the waning light while trudging
homewards with their wives as they had never done
before. Something dimmed their vision besides the
gathering twilight, but the wives, with woman's true tact,
said, "Ay, ay!" as they wiped their own tears away,
which the sight of this bright boy so early orphaned had
caused to flow.

Neither uncle Arthur nor his sister ever went inside a
carriage when they could help it, but they thought the
little town-bred duckling, as Amie called him, might not
be used to night-air; therefore, much to his indignation,
he was stowed away with his French bonne and his
aunt's maid in the omnibus with all the packages, while
his much-to-be-envied relations drove off in a high
phaeton with a pair of very spirited horses.

"When shall I be a man?" he sighed, as he flattened
his nose against the closed window, for the maids, of
course, shut out every breath of air.

"Speak French," said his bonne, who rarely had the
opportunity of tutoring him, and who was naturally not
slow in taking advantage of such rare opportunities.
She was a very little woman, quick-tempered, but kind-
hearted and full of vivacity.

Geoffrey touched his hat in the new style his aunt had
just inculcated, and smiled without answering.

"Do not imitate the bumpkin squires and their serfs,"
the bonne continued. She pronounced the words, which
were untranslatable, so funnily that Geoffrey burst out
laughing. Natalie's literature was confined to the study

of the thrilling romances of the middle ages; she was now going through a course of Sir Walter Scott's novels in English, with the help of a dictionary and the French translations for occasional reference, and she evidently imagined that the feudal system still prevailed in England. Can we picture to ourselves a Yorkshire farmer of this nineteenth century of ours undergoing for one week the active operation of this system ? A French bonne or a London fine lady might call him a serf or a bumpkin, he would touch his hat with perfect indifference; but woe betide the squire who interferes with the privileges of such serfs ! He will give feudal respect and reverence with all the pleasure in life, especially if the squire is the right sort, but woe betide any sort who should interfere with the liberty of the bumpkin.

"What does she mean by boomkeen and cerf?" wondered Geoffrey. "Ah, but I see the stags !" For they were now entering the park, which was so spacious that red deer throve very fairly there. It was undulating, though not actually hilly, and the whole property was extensively wooded. The house did not stand in the park, it was in the very heart of an old-fashioned plaisaunce—no other name conveys the idea of rambling pleasure grounds, labyrinths without end, quaint fishponds, and gardens within gardens.

An avenue of nearly two miles led up to the house; first oak, then elms, near the house birch and limes intermixed with horse-chestnuts and hawthorn trees, making what the garden woman called "May bowers," in the spring.

The rooks were very busy, and were making such a noise that Geoffrey exclaimed, "What is the matter?"

"French, if you please," snapped Natalie.

Again Geoffrey touched his hat, and answered, "It would not be civil to Mrs. Parker."

This speech went straight to Parker's Yorkshire heart, she hated French-fangled ways, as she called them, and she explained that the matter was simply the rookery.

"But what is that?"

Parker pointed upwards and Geoffrey saw the wise black birds settled and settling for the night in the bare branches of the great forest trees which spread so high over his head.

"Birds going to bed, I see," he said. "Are they ravens?"

"Rooks, sir," was the answer. Natalie was in the sulks, her boasted Parisian politeness had been shamed by a little English boy whom she was prepared to esteem a boompkeen. So Geoffrey and Parker benefited, and enjoyed an uninterrupted conversation until they reached the Hall, a great rambling building in various styles of architecture, but forming nevertheless a handsome and stately whole. The ruins of an old castle stood on a slight eminence in the park, visible from the present house; from one of the towers of the castle a bright flag told the neighbours when the family were at home.

The Normans had lived here ever since the Conquest; they came over with William, and they had probably been as rude and as lawless as all the invaders. They

certainly secured a very fair inheritance for their descendants, and Arthur Norman was prouder of being the
oldest untitled gentleman in the county than any mush-
room peer, not born in the purple, can be of his coronet.

For six generations the Normans had declined a title,
and Arthur was not likely to break the spell now.

He and his sister are standing on the steps to receive
Geoffrey, just as if he had been a bride and bridegroom
the old coachman observed ; and the little boy, with the
simple unconsciousness of childhood, walked up the long
flight of steps as naturally as if they led to the London
house he had called home for all his short life.

His Antie kissed him, and his uncle told him with grave
kindness to consider Normanhurst his home for the
future; but the old housekeeper, who had held him in
her arms when he was born, interrupted the uncle's
formal address, and pressing forward she caught the
child to her breast, and kissed him again and again, for
his mother as well as for himself.   A chord was touched
which saved his newly developed boyhood from offence,
and those two became the fastest of friends.

Kind Eleanor noticed the cloud on Natalie's face, and
gave her a special greeting, asked how she was getting on
with " Ivanhoe," and took her upstairs to the bright,
pretty room she had prepared for her.

Geoffrey's little room adjoined his aunt's, which he had
arranged as soon as he knew he was to live with her.
Natalie taught him French, his mother had taught him
everything else.   Uncle Arthur actually came upstairs
to see if Geoffrey liked his quarters, and he said some-

thing civil to the bonne in a language which represented
French to his own mind, and which seemed to satisfy
Natalie ; but Geoffrey whispered to his Amie, " It will not
do for me to talk French with uncle Arthur. I don't
think he would understand me when I *glisser* the words
properly, and I am sure Natalie will say his accent is
détestable."

Whatever she thought on the subject, Natalie did
not gratify her *élève*, as she like to call him, by expressing
her sentiments on the subject of his uncle's pronunciation, and the tea now caused a diversion. A nice room
communicating with Natalie's bedroom was set apart for
Geoffrey and his bonne, and Eleanor pleased them both
by asking for a cup of tea. Uncle Arthur had retired,
having done a great deal more than Eleanor had dared to
hope he would do ; and, though Geoffrey was beginning
to think he was not so bad as he had seemed at first, he
was a long way from being desirable as a constant companion. The tea was very merry, Amie talked French
to set her nephew an example of obedience and discipline,
and she made mistakes on purpose in order to let
Geoffrey see how dutifully and gratefully she accepted
Natalie's corrections. She feigned so well that the bonne
was taken in, and wondered how a lady who spoke with
almost a Parisian accent could be guilty of such gram-
matical blunders. Geoffrey took no apparent notice then,
but when he had finished his prayers he offered up a little
impromptu prayer that "Amie might be quite good, and
not do stories by pretending not to know, when she spoke
French."

The quick colour which always betrayed any emotion flushed Eleanor's cheek. She was young still, and was too charming to be perfect.

She was very generous, like all naturally impetuous people, and. she had the wisdom to acknowledge her fault now in the most frank and engaging manner.

"Dear Geoffrey, I wanted to teach you how to take a reproof nicely, and I quite forgot that I might instead teach you to play with truth."

"Kind Amie," murmured the boy, laying his curly head on her shoulder; "you will never pretend again. You know it·could not teach me to take a reproof well, because when you pretend to make a mistake you don't mind Natalie saying, 'Pardon, Madame, on dit tel ou tel;' but if you really did make a mistake very often it would make you snap just as I do when Natalie calls me 'bête,' and sets me right every other minute. I told her once it was very wrong to say beast, mother never could bear such words, and she says it only means stupid, but I know it means beast too."

Geoffrey had forgotten and forgiven his aunt's little error, but she did not forget it quickly. Long after he was fast asleep she knelt beside his crib and prayed for grace and light not only to guide him aright, but so to order her own deeds and words that she might teach him by example more than by precept.

It was a great responsibility for such a young woman to have the sole charge of a boy with so much cha-racter, for Arthur was not likely to help her much. He seemed to give up everything to her too much as it was, and she was always afraid of becoming masterful and dictatorial. She sometimes feared she liked her life too well. She never took into account the daily anxieties and the real hard work of all sorts that such a life entailed. She could hardly look at her sleeping charge without crying. He was so lovely, and so like the beautiful mother she would never see on earth again, with a touch of his bereaved and lonely father; as she gazed, the whole story of the bygone month came vividly before her.

She passed her fingers through those golden brown rings of curls that clustered over his head, and even in his sleep the action recalled the mother who could never do it again, for he turned round, half-opened his glorious blue eyes, and murmured " Mammy."

She kissed the rosy parted lips, and he settled down again, while she turned away promising herself to be at least his true and faithful *friend*, and to devote her life to him as long as he should need her care.

CHAPTER IV.

THE FIRST DAY.

THE moon was full at about six o'clock in the morning, and it was certainly brighter than many a London day at noon.

Eleanor, a true lover of air and light, always slept with the window and shutter open, winter and summer alike, and she was always up and dressed before most people. Still, excepting on particular occasions, she did not get up by moonlight, and she was sleeping now very comfortably, tired after her journey and all the subsequent emotions and excitements attendant on her arrival at home with her only sister's son.

When she was a child of the same age as Geoffrey, she had been in the habit of walking in her sleep, and Mrs. Norman, her aunt and most motherly guardian, had caused the sides of her crib to be made so high that even with assistance it was no easy matter to get out ; and Eleanor thought this cage-like crib would be the very thing for her nephew, who would be quite capable of walking out of his bed wide-awake, let alone sleep-walking, if any experiments should strike him in the night or early morning which he could practice without delay.

Eleanor had not seen Geoffrey's face when he caught sight of this crib, and he was too polite to express his sentiments on the subject to its purveyor, beyond remarking that it only wanted a door in the side and a roof to make it into a cage. He told Natalie it was very plain that aunt Eleanor had never had any children of her own, but he was too wise to comment to her upon the crib's extraordinary proportions. When she had arranged his clothes he asked her in his best French to put the chair on which they lay close to his bedside, " I like to see them first thing," he explained ; and Natalie was so disarmed by his well-delivered sentences, and by his candour, that for a wonder she complied with his request.

When he woke in the morning he was puzzled as to his whereabouts, and the sides of his cage were so suggestive of a prison that he was inclined to think an already fondly cherished dream of being captured by brigands was fulfilled. Then he began to remember his journey, his arrival at Normanhurst, and so by degrees he recollected where he was.

" I wonder how Amie reached in to kiss me last night, I should have thought only those animals with the necks at the Zoo'gical Gardens "—he was not quite at home with hard words yet—" giraffes—could have managed it. She must have knelt on the chair. I hope to goodness she did not take it away." He sat up to look. No, there was the chair just where Natalie had put it. His clothes were a little tumbled, it was evident that his aunt must have made use of the chair to reach him. The moon was making his room as light as most of the days he had been recently accustomed to, he thought every one must .have overslept themselves, and he was prepared to rouse the household with great glee.

By this time he was on his feet, but very little more than his head and shoulders appeared above the side of the crib. He looked all round, and noticed with great satisfaction that the door between his room and Amie's was ajar. He had great doubts of being able to manage those heavy oak doors and their strong brass handles. But now he must get out of his present prison. " If I can just get one foot over the bar I shall manage ; then I can bring the other leg over, sit on the rail like the little robin-redbreast mother used to sing about, drop on the chair, and once out of this bed no one shall ever put me in again."

While thus conversing with himself, he had been lifting first one sturdy leg and then the other, but hitherto in vain. One rosy toe just touched the bar, with acrobatic skill, but could not even cross it, much less could the foot perform the feat. Quite breathless with exertion, he sat down on his pillow to devise some other means. He looked so lovely with his flushed cheeks and tumbled curly hair, it was a pity Sir Joshua Reynolds, the great painter of old times, did not " walk," as the people would say who believe in ghosts : he might have left a picture on the table which would have enchanted aunt Eleanor. But ghosts never do such sensible things, and there is little hope that Geoffrey would have sat still long enough for even a spirit-painter to catch his likeness.

An idea strikes him. Up he gets, takes hold of one end of his little mattress and tries to lift it. At last he succeeds in getting between the two mattresses, and by that means doubles up the top mattress, creeps up the mountain he has just heaved Atlas-wise on his shoulders, and at last stands where tradition at least never says that hero of mythologic lore stood, on the top of his own mountain.

Geoffrey did not know about Atlas yet, but he would probably learn in time how he was supposed to support the heavens on his shoulders, after being changed into a mountain. There is a mountain called Atlas, which is so high that the ancients imagined it reached the heavens, and this idea, no doubt, gave rise to the fable.

But Geoffrey is now standing on the top of his own mountain, a fact and no fable ; in another minute he is sitting like the robin he had alluded to on the rail, and he was nodding his head at least quite as merrily as the bird in the song ; then plump he comes down on the chair, and patter patter went his bare feet over the floor. He cannot see Amie when he gets into her room, for though she is not caged round, her bed is old fashioned, and consequently very high. But Geoffrey having got out of a cage without wings, was not going to be kept on the floor when he was aiming at the same level as that occupied by his unconscious aunt.

A chair will help him up as it had helped him down, and Eleanor began to dream of fairies, of rustling wings, and then she felt something cold and soft against her face.

She was wide awake in a minute, like all healthy, active-minded, active-natured people.

She could not sit up at first, for a pair of arms are round her neck, and the cold soft something is pressing her head firmly against the pillow. But she finds voice to exclaim,—

"Geoffrey, Geoffrey, you monkey, how on earth did you get here? I thought you were as safe as a mouse in a trap."

"Ah! you should have put a roof on the cage then," he answered, releasing his aunt to see how she looked.

"Very rosy and nice," he observed, answering his own thought.

"Rosy, very," she replied, taking his face in both her hands; "but I don't know whether I think it very nice to be awakened by it at six o'clock in the morning."

"My dear Amie, it *must* be very late. It is *quite* light."

Geoffrey was very emphatic when he saw a prospect of holding a friendly argument.

"You poor little cockney," said Eleanor, "do you call this light? Pale moonlight is not what we put up with in the country. The farmers do not consider it light enough to begin work amongst their cattle by, but strengthen it by means of a lantern. I should have liked another hour's sleep," she continued, turning away and closing her eyes as she spoke.

"I could not possibly shut my eyes again, I want to see everything. Don't you think just for this one morning you could take me out by 'pale moonlight,' with a lantern to help," he said, coaxingly, turning head over heels as he spoke, and bringing his face opposite his aunt's face again quite successfully.

Eleanor certainly had the sweetest temper in the world. She did try to temporise by proposing a good talk where they were, but Geoffrey was on wires, and could not possibly lie or sit still for another minute. So his aunt actually got up, and dropped him back into his cage, where he promised to try and keep still while she dressed herself. She knew Mrs. Parker would not respond to any bell for an hour at the least, and Geoffrey emphatically described Natalie's objection to early rising. After finishing her own toilet as far as her hair, which was quite beyond her control, she proceeded to do for her nephew. He did not much like her very vigorous way of washing him, and he was inclined to resent the cold water vehemently, but she did it all as such a matter of course that he resolutely swallowed his tears, and Eleanor never knew what a little hero he had been when he underwent at her hands the horrors of his first cold tub without even the chill off. By the time he was dressed Mrs. Parker made her appearance, and Eleanor's hair was made fit to be seen, which operation caused Geoffrey to undergo agonies of impatience.

"You would be much prettier, Amie, with hair like mine. I think, as you have got me now, you had better have your hair cut off. I really cannot wait every morning while it is being done."

"Do you suppose," said his aunt, when she could speak for laughing, "that I am going through such a

4

morning as this every day?   No, my dear Geoffrey, we
must come to a fair and full understanding.   You know
when I found you preparing to shave your legs I told
you I could not take care of you unless you helped me
by taking care of yourself.   Now part of the business
of taking care will consist of managing you, and I cannot
do that without your help.   You must manage yourself,
and the best beginning will be to arrange the days.
'All work and no play makes Jack a dull boy,' is a
proverb I think some boy must have invented.   There
is great sense in it; but, on the other hand, 'All play
and no work would make Geoffrey a very unmanageable
boy.'"

"You *are* very mean, Amie.   You might just as well
be cross, because then I should never dream of obeying
you; but when you speak like that you are almost like
mother, except that your eyes look so funny, and
mother's never twinkled as yours do.   They are just like
those stars—not the big still ones, but the ones that
shoot and dance; I always think they must be having
such fun."

Eleanor and Parker were both laughing heartily, and
Parker said,—

"Oh, dear me, Miss Norman, we shall never get you
married now.   You always said you should like a little
boy without a husband, and now you have got one, and
a handful, too."

"What's that?" said Geoffrey.   "Amie married?
Why isn't she married to uncle Arthur?"

"She belongs to him, and you belong to us both," said

Eleanor. "And now come along. We will have no discipline to-day. It is Saturday, which is always more or less of a holiday; then comes Sunday, and we will begin on Monday as we mean to go on."

Children do sometimes find that there is sufficient good in particular days for ample content. Geoffrey was in no hurry for Monday; he would have been glad enough for Saturday to go on for certainly a whole year, and he did not even wish to be an hour older. He had never had any playfellows of his own age, his parents would not allow him to go to children's parties; and though he was allowed to play with children in the square and in the park, he generally preferred his own company. He always drove with his mother whenever he could, and walked with his father; their society was more delightful than his own, and of course they were far before Natalie.

But in all his short happy experience of life he had never enjoyed such a day as this wonderful Saturday.

It was one of those exceptional days that only come in February, and rarely enough then. The sun shone all day, the sky was as blue as Geoffrey's eyes, and nothing could be bluer than they were; the birds began to sing with all their might, the snowdrops looked as if they would like to lift up their drooping heads, so widely did they separate their three snowy petals in order to let the sun reach their yellow hearts. The primrose-stars stared right up at the sky, coming out in a magical way with hardly a green leaf of their own to boast of, so anxious were they to do homage to the beauty of the

4 *

day. The catkins danced about, shedding their yellow powder on the bright little brushes of deep red which would be nuts in the autumn. The rooks cawed unceasingly, dropping sticks all over the place in their hurry to get their nests finished. In short, it was a grand day for Geoffrey to make his first acquaintance with country sights and sounds, and many a hearty laugh did his aunt enjoy at his expense during its progress. But it will take a whole chapter to introduce Geoffrey to the house and grounds, and so we will leave him for the present at breakfast with his uncle and aunt in a room which was called the small dining-room in that great rambling place, but which seemed much too large in Geoffrey's eyes for three people.

CHAPTER V.

COUNTRY LIFE.

In spite however of its size, the small dining - room was very cheerful. The morning sun looked in at the large windows and touched up Eleanor's bright hair till it shone like gold. It had no respect for uncle Arthur's grave face, but rippled up and down his features as fearlessly as it did all over Geoffrey. The little fellow had politely declined a high chair which had been turned out of some lumber-room, and polished up for his use ; consequently, not much more than his face appeared above the level of the table.

But he assured Amie it had been found to be the best way for eating purposes—" I have never fed my pinafore once since I have had a proper chair ; " and certainly he was eating his bread and milk in a way that left nothing to be desired.

Arthur and his sister always breakfasted at half-past eight ; there was never company to disturb this excellent arrangement, and, to that sister's surprise, Arthur himself proposed that Geoffrey should always breakfast with them. His dinner of course would fit in with their luncheon, and he and his Amie would have their tea

together. Uncle Arthur did not patronise that meal,
though he did occasionally find his way into the music-
room when Eleanor was having her own solitary cup, and
ask for one for himself. There would be no more solitude now for Eleanor, and the prospect seemed to have
added an extra touch of brightness to her always bright
face and cheery pleasant voice. After breakfast she went
to the housekeeper's room, and did not make believe,
but really did look into all the household matters. Then
she went on to the kitchen, a sight to be seen in its spotless order, and there she arranged about luncheon and
dinner, and ordered Master Geoffrey's tea with her own
for the future. " Bread and milk, and rather more bread
and butter than I get through alone," she said. Every one
looked happy in that well-ordered, well-regulated household, and the gravest face lighted up with some reflection
of her own smiles when Miss Norman approached.
Geoffrey was following his aunt, taking in everything,
and approving entirely of all he saw. When this necessary portion of her morning's work was over, Eleanor
turned to her patient follower, and said, " Now, Geoffrey,
for this one day I am going to amuse you entirely ; what
shall we do first ? "

" Go all over the house," was the prompt answer.

So Amie led him through all the state apartments,
which were shown once a week to the public : the great
banqueting hall hung round with armour and other relics
of bygone times ; the grand saloon or withdrawing-room,
the lesser withdrawing-room, both rooms full of family
portraits, from the stiff caricatures of early times, square

and flat as a child's first attempt, down to the dark Van-dykes, the Sir Peter Lelys, and the perfect pictures of Sir Joshua Reynolds, and his immediate predecessors and successors. There was a picture of a little boy by the great painter Angela Kaufmann, hung low down, which was so like Geoffrey that he himself started back, thinking that he had come to a looking-glass, and that the fairies had been at work with his clothes, changing his homespun and spotless collar into deep coloured velvet, and yellow lace ruffles.

"That is your great-grandfather," said his aunt; "you certainly are wonderfully like him." The boy had been too much interested to talk much at first, but now that his aunt had broken the magic spell of interested silence he fired off a perfect volley of questions.

His aunt was fortunately well versed in the traditions of the place, and she could tell him the history of every picture and the special association connected with each room.

At last they came to the suite of apartments which had been graced by the presence of more than one monarch. Charles I. in the happy days of his prosperity had spent a week at Normanhurst with his queen, and the Normans had always protected the Stuarts until they were finally driven out of the land. They were as canny as they were loyal, those old Normans; they never lost an acre through their loyalty. There was a certain coolness during the reigns of the two first Georges, but George III. had thought it well, in their case, to forgive and forget, and had honoured the reigning Normans with a visit. The grand old squire hardly appreciated the honour, and was loth to put the "old German," as he called him, into the grim state bedroom where Charles I. had slept. But Lady Eleanor, his wife, was the daughter of a courtier, she recognised secretly the divine right of kings, which had cost Charles I. his throne and his head, and thanks to the good dame King George had a right royal welcome. Besides, Mr. Norman was a Yorkshireman, which is another word for a prince of hospitality, and the homely nature of the king completely disarmed his host.

"But we shall never get out-of-doors to-day," said aunt Eleanor, who had been delighting her nephew with these royal details. "I will just show you the rooms where uncle Arthur and I live generally, and then we will come and see the stables and the farm and the gardens."

They had now reached the ordinary hall, a charming room lined with oak, and fitted up with old-fashioned furniture, high-backed chairs, a quaint carved settle, dogs and a wide hearth instead of a modern fireplace; and the windows were set very deep, with old coats-of-arms let in, which repeated themselves on the dark polished floor in many-coloured hues. There was an organ at one end, and the hall was open to the top of the house, so that it was a grand place for music. The small dining-room where they had breakfasted was on one side, another door led into uncle Arthur's study; then came Eleanor's own sitting-room, where she and her brother usually sat in the evening, unless he wanted to hear the

organ, which his sister played with more than common
power. On these occasions he seemed to forget his sorrow, and Eleanor played for hours until she was worn
out from sheer fatigue, but as long as he looked
peaceful she went on playing. The bellows were worked
by water, so there was no human victim required to blow.
Eleanor's sitting-room must be particularly described
later, Geoffrey hardly noticed it now as he ran through
it to fetch his hat and coat; he little knew how familiar it
would become to him in the future.

The stables were even more enchanting than the house.
Aunt Eleanor's two ponies that she drove seemed to
know her quite well, the horses she and uncle Arthur
rode were equally friendly, and as to the old stud groom,
his face shone like his horses' coats, and they were bright,
when he caught sight of Miss Norman. Every stable-
boy about the place looked the better for a sight of her,
and Geoffrey was delighted by their funny remarks.

"Not a little bit," said Wilkinson, the old coachman,
when she asked if he thought her new pet would take
the place of her old dumb friends; "there's isn't such a
thing." By which he meant that Eleanor could not do
such a thing as forsake old friends for new.

"And now to put the young master on the Sheltie Mr.
Arthur got t'oother day." The old servants had not taken
to the habit of styling their present master Mr. Norman;
he did not notice such things, and Eleanor liked to hear
the familiar name from their faithful lips.

Geoffrey had ridden in London, and the old groom
was satisfied with his good seat and generally fearless de-

meanour. Arthur came up at this moment, and he actually smiled upon his nephew.

"Good will come out of evil," said the privileged servant. "Missus and I, we have been bad since we heard that Miss Marian was away, but if losing her gives master back his old brightness we munna grudge Miss Marian the good she's surely gotten."

And Eleanor nodded kindly as she turned away her head so that neither Arthur nor Geoffrey might see her tears. She was not ashamed of them, but she always liked to smile for others and hide her own sorrow.

Arthur actually went on to the Home Farm with the aunt and nephew, and he nearly fell down, he laughed so heartily over Geoffrey's remarks. "What a funny noise that chicken is making." "That chicken" was the sultan of the farmyard crowing a challenge to a young cockerel who had defied him. "And, oh, look at the things that rustle and gobble with those horrid rags hanging round their heads."

The turkey-cock seemed to understand that he was being insulted, and made such a rush at Master Geoffrey that our hero retired behind his aunt.

It would be impossible to describe Geoffrey's surprise, or to detail all his cockney remarks; aunt Eleanor's tears ran down her cheeks unchecked and unconcealed, they were the result of her hearty laughter. Geoffrey was too much taken up with all the strange sights and sounds to notice, much less to resent his relatives' merriment, and the morning came to an end quite too quickly for the three.

After luncheon Amie drove him in her pretty low

pony-carriage, and actually let him hold the reins when they came to a very straight piece of the road. She had several visits to pay, and she and Geoffrey had tea with a certain Mary, who kissed him very warmly and cried over him. She had been nurse to his mother and aunt, and now she was a prosperous farmer's wife, with a lot of nurslings of her own; but she had love and to spare for this orphaned child of her first nursling. Her house was not far from the Hall, so Eleanor sent her carriage home, and she and Geoffrey walked back by starlight.

That night when he had finished his prayers he said, "Amie, I don't miss mother as much as I expected. I think I ought to try and miss her a little more, so please don't make me quite so happy, at least for a few days. I do miss her a little, and I want her now to tell her about to-day. You see, I cannot tell you because you know, and I don't care to tell Natalie, it would be such a bore to say it in French. Do you think she knows about to-day?"

Again Eleanor's tears rose to her eyes, but the gloom concealed them, and she was able to answer after a scarcely perceptible pause.

"It is very nice to think she does know that you are happy. I like to think that her bright spirit watches us and prays for us. And now, darling, let me drop you into your cage, and please don't get out of it until Natalie comes, for I am beginning to feel thus early in the evening that you have done me out of an hour at least of my proper sleep."

At dinner with her brother she concealed all trace of weariness, however, and talked so brightly that he wondered of her, as she had wondered of Geoffrey, whether she had very deep feelings.

Poor Arthur thought true feeling was best expressed by gravity and gloom. Eleanor never allowed her feelings to affect other people, and she had so trained herself that she was always able, not only to appear, but to be cheerful under any circumstances.

After dinner the choir came into the Hall to practise for the next day's services, and, contrary to his custom, Arthur came in when the little party were at work and not likely to notice him.

The hymns Eleanor chose touched upon their recent loss, but the words were cheering and the tunes were bright. She would fain that all should see beyond the present sorrow, and her voice rang out clearly when the strong men's faltered, as she sang Faber's lovely hymn,—

> Brighter still and brighter
> Glows the western sun,
> Shedding all its gladness
> On our work that's done.
> Time will soon be over,
> Toil and sorrow past ;
> May we, blessed Saviour,
> Find a rest at last.

Eleanor did not see her brother again that night, and when she hung over Geoffrey's crib she was able to relieve her own feelings. She cried quietly for some time, until the sight of his smiling peaceful repose soothed her, and she was soon sleeping as calmly, and far more dreamlessly than he was.

CHAPTER VI.

AT CHURCH.

ELEANOR was having her hair done on Sunday morning when a little tap came at her door, and, scarcely waiting for a cheerful "come in," Geoffrey darted into the room.

"Amie, dear, if I promise not to get out unless I have a real good reason, will you let me have a bed like my own in London? I cannot bear that cage. I should never dream of walking in my sleep, and if I don't get up when I am awake till it is time there is no need to put me into that cage."

Eleanor laughingly promised to find him another bed on Monday if he would endure his cage patiently for one night more, and then she took him on her knee and asked for one of his prettiest hymns.

Then Parker, having finished dressing her mistress, went off to her breakfast, and Eleanor and her nephew had a little private conversation. Directly after breakfast she had to go to the school, and as Geoffrey wished to go to morning service she left him with his uncle, who volunteered to take care of him until church-time, to Eleanor's delighted surprise. Geoffrey laid himself out to entertain his uncle, and proposed a walk round the garden.

"Why don't you teach in the school?" he began.

After a somewhat awkward pause Arthur answered, "There are plenty without me."

"And besides," continued Geoffrey, with a child's pleasant tact, "you have got me to take care of now. Will you tell me all you know about the gardens, please—who made them—and about the ladies in funny clothes walking about ever so long ago? Amie had not time yesterday. She only told me a very little about the house. She knows lots more."

Uncle Arthur did not know that his romance-loving sister had spoken her thoughts aloud as she led her nephew through the long corridors and stately rooms of the old Hall.

She had spoken of ladies in stiff brocades and high-heeled shoes, moving about or sitting at their tapestry and their spinning, with their maidens around them. She had made the cavaliers of the court of Charles I. live again, until the little boy had dreamed he was one himself; and now he wanted uncle Arthur to take up the dropped thread of his aunt's tale and pull the strings for these ladies and gentlemen of the past, in order that they might promenade for him in the quaint, old-fashioned garden, where they would certainly have not seemed out of place.

Luckily the ringing-in bell of the church, which was close by, took the place of the lovely chimes which had been going on for the last half-hour, and Arthur got out of his difficulty by telling his nephew that it was church-time.

The organ and choir were in the proper place, thanks to aunt Eleanor, and the chancel was altogether a credit to any church, even to the beautiful church itself, which was the pride of the place. But the rest of the extensive building was decidedly barn-like in its arrangements, and the pews were like nothing so much as cattle pens, some large and some small.

The Hall pew was like a room, extremely comfortable with its well-cushioned corners and its soft hassocks. But Geoffrey, who had been accustomed to the rigid discomfort of a London church, which was connected in his mind with reverent behaviour, gazed round in such astonishment that he forgot to kneel down and say his prayer to himself. Uncle Arthur looked into his hat so earnestly for a minute that Geoffrey stood up on tip-toe in order to look in too. "Have you got anything curious?" he asked, which made Arthur look inside harder than ever; the question quite upset his gravity. "Well?" continued Geoffrey, getting on to the seat in his eagerness and peering as well as he could over his uncle's shoulder.

The voluntary fortunately began at this moment, and music always had a soothing effect on the eager impetuous nature as upon the gloomier disposition of the uncle. Both were composed to due gravity by the time the service began.

The old rector, who had christened Geoffrey and his mother before him, had rather a peculiar delivery. He was very charming out of church, and his manner to children was particularly engaging. But he read in a very funny, old-fashioned way, and Geoffrey, who was used to the monotone, was up on the seat again to inspect this new phenomenon. " Is he doing it to make me laugh?" he asked, with a smile dimpling all over his eager face.

"Certainly not," said uncle Arthur, who with the eyes of rector and congregation upon him felt that he must be stern. "I am afraid I shall have to, though," he continued, after a really laudable effort to compose his features.

"Will you ask him not to speak so funnily then." Geoffrey's whisper was getting louder and louder in his eagerness, and all eyes were now turned on the Hall pew. "I might be gooder with Amie," said Geoffrey, in answer to a really pathetic remonstrance from Arthur. "You look nearly as funny as the old gentleman talks. I think I am going to laugh quite loud in a minute."

Fortunately it was time to kneel down, and equally fortunately, Arthur thought, the door of the pew led into the chancel. "Come to Amie," he said, using Geoffrey's name in his agitation; as a rule he set his face against pet names.

"It will be best I think." And in another minute he was inclosed with his aunt, out of sight though not out of hearing.

She understood in a moment what had happened, but she did not even look at Geoffrey. The service was all choral, and so her time and attention were fully occupied.

It was a real case of behind-the-scenes for the boy, and he was quite interested in all the mysteries which had such pleasant results in this case outside, for Eleanor played beautifully, and her choir was really first-rate.

The old clergyman did not read the lessons, and Geoffrey had almost forgotten him, when he became audible again by himself reading the gospel. Being unable to see, Geoffrey quite forgot he could be heard, and he asked in a clear penetrating voice,—

" *Why does* the old gentleman speak in that funny way, Amie ? "

. He was more emphatic than usual, and there was an audible titter from the choir boys. The men behaved admirably ; and Eleanor looked at Geoffrey without any twinkle in her eyes, and so reproachfully that his own eyes filled with tears, and he was quite still for the rest of the service.

A stranger preached, who riveted the attention of every one, and Geoffrey was as interested as the oldest person present. The sermon was very short and very simple, but so earnest and so much to the point that the words went straight to every heart.

The text was, " To me to live is Christ, and to die is gain." The old rector had not been able to trust himself to preach on the subject that was occupying all thoughts in that neighbourhood ; and this stranger, who had not known her, was able to treat the subject in a general way, but still with such point that Geoffrey whispered, while the rector in a trembling voice pronounced the blessing, " He has been reminding every one of mother."

Amie pressed his hand and he knew that he was forgiven for his earlier indiscretion. Every one went out of

5

church before Eleanor left the organ. Geoffrey listened entranced as she played a solemn strain suitable to the occasion. At the church-door the rector's wife was waiting for her.

"Come in for a few minutes," she said, after they had exchanged greetings. "The rector has a plan to unfold, and he wants to introduce you to his favourite, Edward Chamberlayne."

The name seemed familiar to Miss Norman, but the face had recalled nothing to her memory as she had watched him, unseen, from her quiet corner.

Geoffrey and the rector made friends at once; he said funny things in his funny voice which the boy felt there was no need to ask leave to laugh at; and Amie and Mr. Chamberlayne were soon talking quite as busily, but in a graver strain.

Edward Chamberlayne was working hard in a very poor London parish, his salary was small, and his private means were modest in the extreme. He was married and he had four little delicate children who were all sadly in want of country air. The rector of Norman-hurst, who enjoyed a large private fortune which he spent nobly, was bent on doing his favourite a good turn. Though he and his wife were both sixty, they enjoyed perfect health, and he was going to fulfil an old promise of many years' standing, this very coming spring, of taking her the grand tour of Italy, Switzerland, and Germany. He proposed leaving Edward Chamberlayne in charge of his parish during his absence, and, with unpa-ralleled generosity, giving up to him during the time the net income of the large stipend he received. His living was the largest in the county, and the work was comparatively light. This was the plan the rector was going to unfold to Eleanor, and he was pleased to see how well the pair were already getting on. " Will you and Arthur come in after evening service ?" he said, when he told Eleanor what he was going to do; " I should like to have my patron's sanction. Don't say what I want him for, but tell him he must come in on business. You will like Mrs. Chamberlayne quite as much as you already seem to like Edward, and the children will be nice companions for this young man."

Arthur refused to go in to the rectory when he heard there was a stranger, though he had. evidently been impressed with Mr. Chamberlayne's sermon, but he raised no objection to the rector's wish about the proposed arrangement.

Eleanor did not go in either, for she never allowed her brother to spend a lonely evening if she could help it, and after Geoffrey had gone to bed she drew a low chair beside his and tried to engage him in conversation. He answered her sometimes when she appealed to him in a direct manner, but for the most part he let her go on talking and did not seem to hear what she said.

He brightened up a little when she alluded to Geoffrey, and he even volunteered an account of his experiences in church, so that, altogether, Eleanor hoped that by degrees her brother might shake off his gloom, and realise that there was a great deal left for him to make life not only bearable but enjoyable.

5 *

Monday morning was to begin the life of discipline for Geoffrey, judiciously mingled with pleasure, which was to keep him bright and cheerful, and yet help to make him wise.

While Eleanor attended to her household duties, he was to do his French lesson with Natalie. Then he was to take a walk with the bonne. After that he was to do half an hour's work with Eleanor, and then to amuse himself quietly until luncheon-time. Eleanor would always take him out in the afternoon, when she could manage it, and after tea when she was not too busy she would devote an hour to his amusement; besides all this, he was at liberty to secure any attention from uncle Arthur that he was willing to afford.

Natalie was the only thorn in his rose-strewn path. She really was more than a crumpled rose-leaf to him, and she certainly was the only person who could make him really naughty. Still she was trustworthy, and she both spoke and taught French well; besides, Marian had wished her to remain, so that Eleanor could not make a change without real cause.

She reasoned with Geoffrey on the subject, and she did not leave him much with the bonne, so that the storms between Geoffrey and Natalie only occurred at intervals.

CHAPTER VII.

MISCHIEF.

ONCE more the scene changes to London. But this time we find ourselves in a part of London which is not generally familiar. Edward Chamberlayne is returning to his parish and to his present home, with the glad news that at least a whole spring and summer and winter of country life is before the sweet patient wife, and the pale though beautiful children.

The vicarage was a handsome-enough house, but it was far too large for the very limited stipend awarded to the vicar of this extremely populous parish. It had doubtless been in days gone by, before the City grandees in imitation of the aristocrats in the West of London made a change of abode, the residence of some wealthy citizen of worship and renown, who, like John Gilpin, had done so well behind the counter that he could afford to panel the walls cf his private house with fine black oak, decorate his ceilings, and carve his chimney-pieces.

The ceilings were very black now, but the decorations were still quite perfect: the panels and carvings would have fetched a sum that might have made the vicar's salary a little less out of proportion with his work and with his wants.

As Edward opens the door with his latch-key, a lovely little girl of five years old springs into his arms and kisses him again and again; a boy of four, who though pale, like all town-bred children, looked healthy enough, embraced his father's legs so vehemently that Mr. Chamberlayne nearly lost his balance as he held out a disengaged hand to a wee boy who could just walk.

"And how are mother and baby?" he asks, after returning his children's loving kisses with warm interest. "Such flowers, and such vegetables, children, and such news! But mother must hear first."

In a pretty oak-panelled room, which might have been the private parlour of a frugal Dame Gilpin, Mrs. Chamberlayne was lying on an old carved settle near the fire, with a little sleeping baby in her arms.

The first impression produced at sight of Lilian Chamberlayne was one of intense loveableness: the usual exclamation of strangers was, "How lovely she is!" And she was as good as she was beautiful. Scarcely as bright as Eleanor Norman, but calmly, evenly cheerful, always thinking for others, though perhaps more capable of showing them how to act than of acting for them. She did her own duty most thoroughly, but where Eleanor did others' work for them Lilian showed them how to work, and in some subtle way made them do their own.

When her husband came in her tender face lighted up with so much joy that he could only respond at first to such a welcome by lavish endearments. "And now for my news, little wife. Mr. Russell is going abroad for the whole spring and summer and winter, and I am to take charge of his parish, and receive all his large tithes."

Lilian could not look brighter than she had looked at the first sight of her husband, but she smiled on contentedly, with his hand in hers, while he enlarged upon all the advantages before them. The rectory and village were called Hurst, shortly and simply, and recalled no memories of the only trouble Lilian had ever known in her bright cherished girlhood. She had been Arthur Norman's chosen bride; he had met her when he was an Oxford undergraduate, and he had loved her before he knew who she was. She liked him very much, and they had been friends for four years before he asked her to be his wife. She mistook friendship for love, and said yes without realising all it entailed. Arthur was intensely happy till within a week of the wedding day, but by that time Lilian had found out the difference between calm friendship and passionate love. Arthur found it out too, and he released her from her promise with thoughtful consideration. "But we will still be friends, Arthur," she said, holding up her face to him as if he had been her brother. He gave her one last kiss, such as the tenderest brother never bestowed on a sister, and when a year later she met Edward Chamberlayne she knew what Arthur's feelings for her had been like. Her parents objected to her marriage with so poor a man, but when they saw her heart was set upon it they consented, unwillingly, to this transplanting of their beautiful country flower to the close atmosphere of London. She had never regretted the step. Children had come quickly, and the purse was very shallow; but help came from many quarters, and now, when affairs were at the worst, this delightful offer came from Edward's old friend, the present rector of Hurst, who had been his father's dearest friend, and who loved Edward for his own sake as well as for the sake of his father's memory.

Perhaps the only resentful feeling Eleanor had ever entertained in her kindly heart had been towards the girl who had blighted her brother's life. They had never met, and Arthur had never told how it had come about, so that Eleanor could only draw her own conclusions. Marian had once met Lilian at an Oxford commemoration, and had lost her heart at once, like every other man, woman, or child who only saw her without speaking to her. Lilian for her part said if Arthur had been like Marian she should have been able to love him quite as much as he loved her. But, doubtless for a wise and good reason, affairs were not to be as Arthur wished.

Even at the risk of material injury to her own and her children's health, she would have stayed in London rather than have paraded her happiness and her husband's content under poor Arthur's eyes. But Hurst conveyed nothing to her mind, and Yorkshire was like a kingdom. She knew Arthur Norman's home was somewhere in that county, but she had never seen it; indeed, she had never been in Yorkshire at all. Edward spoke warmly of Eleanor, but he had unaccountably forgotten the squire's name.

"Indeed, my dear, now I come to think of it, I never heard the surname. The squire I only saw in church, a handsome gloomy-looking man, who evidently could not manage his little son."

And then Edward gave a humorous account of the scene in the church. "The organ was beautifully played by the squiress, and the choir is good beyond a very high average. She and her little boy came into the rectory after morning service. She is very pretty, with such a bright joyous face it was hard to believe she had lately lost her only and dearly loved sister. At the same. time her manner did not give me the impression of any want of feeling; and she is, according to Mrs. Russell, the most purposeful, practical woman in the world."

This was Edward's impression of the inhabitants of Normanhurst. There was a dignity of manner about Miss Norman, in spite of her activity and her light-hearted manner and ways, which gave strangers the impression that she was a young British matron. If only she could have been Arthur's wife instead of his sister, she would probably long ago have shaken him out of his moroseness.

Mrs. Chamberlayne teased her husband about his ignorance of the squire's name and place; and she only said, " How like a man ! " when he suggested that the place might be Hurst Hall.

"More like a woman," suggested Edward, mischievously, determined not to be hen-pecked. "Jumping to a conclusion. They always speak of the Hall, the rectory is Hurst Rectory, and the village is called Hurst ; so that it is more than probable that the squire's place has given the name to village and rectory."

"Most unlikely," said Lilian, womanlike determined to have the last word. "It would be so confusing to have no distinction between the Hall and rectory."

Here the matter was dropped, and for the next few weeks there was so much to do in preparing for the great move that neither husband nor wife had time for playful discussions.

Meanwhile Geoffrey was settling very nicely, on the whole, at Normanhurst. He and Natalie had a desperate quarrel one day, which caused so much merriment that Eleanor feared she had hardly given the bonne the support to which she really was entitled. Arthur gave his nephew a garden for himself, and all the necessary tools on a miniature scale. Of course the gardeners kept the said garden in order, but Geoffrey was very indefatigable. One day, after an unusually busy morning's work, Natalie had seated herself to rest for a few minutes on a very low garden seat, while Geoffrey put his tools away. His watering-pot was full of water, he was going to pour it out, when it suddenly struck him that water made things grow. His seeds were already coming up, they would some of them be tall plants in time. The lowness of Natalie's stature was a great trouble to him, as she could reach very little higher than he could. Indeed, he could reach things by jumping that were quite out of her reach, for Natalie had no spring in her at all. Aunt Eleanor's tall graceful figure was much more to his taste. His mother had been tall too; he thought he might like Natalie better if she were not so dumpy. Her back was towards him. There was a little block of wood behind her. Mounted on this he was on a comfortable level with her head.

Before she knew where she was the whole contents of the watering-pot had completely drenched her. At first she attributed the phenomenon to a sudden and violent shower, but Geoffrey's voice undeceived her as he observed in his best French,—

"Voilà, Natalie, cela vous fera croître peut-être. Je ferai cela tous les jours."

She turned round in a tremendous passion and made a dart at the boy, intending, doubtless, to give him a sound, and not undeserved shaking; but he was too quick for her, he eluded her grasp and darted off in the direction of the house. His motions always reminded his aunt of a butterfly, for his feet hardly touched the ground, while Natalie ran after him like an Irish cow.

"Amie!" he exclaimed, tumbling headlong into her lap as she laid aside her work and held out her arms to him, "I have been watering Natalie with my watering-pot full of water, to try and make her grow, and I promised to do it every day, and, instead of saying 'thank you' to me, she is running after me, looking just like one of those little fat bulls that you say we eat"—he meant bullocks—"and she has got her head down—and here she comes!"

Certainly, Geoffrey's description of her was very graphic, and Eleanor could hardly compose her countenance and bring herself to listen with proper sympathy to Natalie's story.

"Ah, le petit monstre," she began. "Pardon, madame, but just see! I am *abimée*, drowned, and I shall have the fever of rheumatics, and I shall die."

However, Eleanor consoled her as best she could, and persuaded her to go and change her wet things.

Unfortunately she met Arthur, and insisted on explaining her condition to the master. Instead of sympathising, he burst out laughing, which so affronted Natalie that she never called him anything, for some time to come, but the "boompkeen Anglais."

Eleanor was trying to lecture Geoffrey when Arthur came in laughing so heartily that his sister could no longer support her assumed character of monitress, and Master Geoffrey felt quite a hero, besides being complete master of the position.

"Eleanor," said Arthur, after they had done laughing, "I want you to go with me to Short's farm this afternoon ; there is a bother there which you must help me to investigate, and I am going to try a new horse, so we had better not take Geoffrey."

"Very well," was the bright answer, but she did not trust herself to look at her nephew, who, on his part, had considerable difficulty in swallowing his tears at the prospect of an afternoon with Natalie, especially under existing circumstances.

But Amie took his hand, though she carefully avoided looking at him, while she went on talking to Arthur, and the silent sympathy helped little Geoffrey to be brave. Trifles make up the sum of joy and woe for older children, for men and women indeed, and Geoffrey deserved great credit for bearing what was, after all, no trifle in his small experiences of pleasant and unpleasant afternoons.

CHAPTER VIII.

A NEW RECTOR, AN OLD FRIEND.

THE expedition to the farm did not take long, and the new horse went capitally. Arthur drove well, and Eleanor did not know what it was to be afraid. She was a perfectly fearless woman, almost too fearless, and yet she was by no means hard or unfeeling. And though she was never nervous, she was full of sympathy, and if " less winning soft, less amiably mild " than Marian, the poet Wordsworth, who wrote such a charming account of what a woman should be, would have recognised Eleanor as one of the right sort. She was talking now so merrily about the quarrel at the farm, which she had just skilfully settled, that Arthur was obliged to be amused in spite of himself. It was beginning to strike him that he had cherished his grief in a morbid unwholesome manner, if the way in which Geoffrey Gordon's father bore his trouble was indeed the right way to meet and to accept sorrow. Eleanor was talking so busily that she did not notice two little figures by the roadside, but as the carriage passed she heard a cry, and looking round she saw something flying along as if either pursued or pursuing.

It was a case of both. Geoffrey had thought it would
be very nice to get rid of Natalie for the rest of the walk,
and felt sure if he could catch the carriage his uncle and
aunt would take him up. Natalie, who had flattered herself that, whatever Geoffrey might think, he really was " en
penitence" for his morning's freak, was determined that
he should undergo the full spell and finish the walk,
which he certainly took too little pains to conceal was
most distasteful to him.

But Natalie might as well try to catch one of
those many-hued dragon-flies which in a few months
would dart round and flit across the ponds in the
garden. Geoffrey came up to the side of the phaeton, neither flushed nor out of breath, just as his uncle
pulled up. There were tears in his eyes, though,
for he could not understand his Amie passing him
without a glance, and he began to fear he really was
in disgrace. But both the smiling faces now looking
down upon him reassured him, as Amie desired the
groom to help him up. Little enough help he required,
and no second bidding, and he was comfortably settled
between Arthur and Eleanor, when Natalie came pound-
ing and panting up.

Eleanor apologised for robbing her of her companion,
and asked her if she would like to get in behind. Now
Natalie was divided between the difficulty of the ascent,
and the danger of walking alone in a country lane, and
she could not make up her mind which of the two evils
was the least. Arthur, thinking his sister's invitation had
not been plain enough, seconded it in his best French—a

most literal translation of what he would have said in his own tongue.

"Levez-vous au dos" (get up at the back). He perhaps thought she expected room to be made in front. With the groom's help she was got in at the back, Geoffrey watching the operation with great interest.

"Is she very heavy, Wilson? Hold her tight, and don't mind if she screams. There, how do you like it, Natalie?" And then the carriage was in motion again, and Geoffrey had a good deal to reveal. In the first place he wanted to know whether it was the manly way of inviting a person to get into a carriage, "'Levez-vous au dos.' Natalie says, 'Levez-vous,' when she wants me to get up from my chair, or out of bed. But when she wants me to get up in that way she would say, 'Montez, montez toujours.' But I daresay she is quite wrong," suggested her pupil in a hopeful voice.

Eleanor was laughing, and even uncle Arthur smiled at his own expense as he answered,—

"I am sure Natalie is right. I was a very naughty boy when I was your age, and I would not learn French. Now that I am grown up I am sorry, as when I travelled in France I found it very inconvenient not being able to speak properly, so you must not imitate my bad example, but take all the advantage you can of Natalie's instructions."

Geoffrey listened politely, but when his uncle had finished speaking, he said, "I am sorry you were wrong, because I meant to say what you said next time I had a chance, and then I should have told Natalie you had said it. Do you know what she calls you, uncle Arthur? I am not sure that I can say it right. Natalie, what is it you call uncle Arthur?"

Natalie's colour had been already heightened by her run after Geoffrey, and her subsequent difficulties in getting into the carriage, but she had been pale then compared to her complexion at this unexpected attack. "Taisez-vous, Monsieur Geoffrey. It is not polite to praise people to their faces."

"Oh! but you didn't praise him, you called him a—a— I have it—a 'boompkeen Anglais.'" Natalie nearly fell out of the carriage; indeed, the groom had to put his arm round her little ball-like person or she really might have rolled out. Eleanor almost screamed, she laughed so heartily, and Arthur all-but lost the reins. He laughed more than he did over the collision of noses in the train; indeed, he laughed as he had not done since his boyhood; and Natalie and Wilson laughed too, the merriment was so infectious. Geoffrey was quite ready to laugh at anything, though he did not see the point of the particular joke which seemed to tickle every one, and altogether the drive ended merrily. Natalie was not going to escape during her descent. Geoffrey posted himself to watch her get down from her elevated seat. "I see more than your feet, Natalie," he exclaimed. "What you call your— what is 'veau' in English? Just above your ankle? I think you had better let two of them lift you. She can't jump or spring a bit, not a little bit," he added, quoting a phrase he had heard the old coachman use, "and I should think she is a good weight though she is so short."

At last Natalie was landed on the ground safely, and she determined in her secret heart never to be in such an elevated position again. She bore Geoffrey's remarks very good-naturedly, so that he informed his aunt while they enjoyed their tea together that there really was not any harm in Natalie.

She, on her part, when she found that Mr. Norman bore no malice, came to the conclusion that though he was a 'boompkeen Anglais,' it was not his fault, and he certainly was not malicious, as were Frenchmen sometimes.

"But, oh! his French," she thought to herself: "who can have had the dishonour of being his teacher?"

The happy weeks went by, and Mr. and Mrs. Russell had started on their grand tour, to Geoffrey's great regret. He liked Mr. Russell thoroughly, and wondered now how he could have thought him funny at church. He liked his sermons, and he loved his stories. They worked together in each other's gardens, and altogether Geoffrey resented the arrival of the Chamberlaynes, in spite of the little companions he was told he might expect.

"You see I am not used to children," he explained; "I never know what to say to them."

Mrs. Chamberlayne and the children arrived on a certain Saturday night; Mr. Chamberlayne had arrived the previous Thursday, but he had not met the Normans, as he was too busy to call. Arthur was in no hurry to make a new acquaintance, and was just as likely as not to omit the ceremony of calling altogether, and Eleanor

6

knew that the lady had not arrived, so that the two
families saw each other for the first time in church.
Eleanor saw Mrs. Chamberlayne in the rectory pew,
with a child on either side of her, as she herself passed
up the chancel with Geoffrey by her side.

"What a dear face," thought Miss Norman.

" How comfor'ble they look," whispered Geoffrey, as
he settled himself in the little corner Amie had arranged
for him.   Whenever Geoffrey attacked the word comfortable he came to grief; his aunt gently whispered,
"Comfor*ta*ble. Very, and so good and quiet;" which hint
acted most beneficially upon Geoffrey, who was determined not to be *out*-good-behaved by the new comers,
so that his conduct left nothing to be desired during the
whole service.   Mrs. Chamberlayne thought as she
watched Eleanor and Geoffrey, " What a charming face
and what a graceful figure !   But she is not Mrs. anything.   How could dear, blind old Edward take her for
the squiress and that bonny boy's mother ? "

But now Lilian's thoughts are most unpleasantly distracted.   She looks towards the squire's pew, and for one
painful moment she meets Arthur's fixed and astonished
eyes.   Her own fall first, but after that glance he never
looks again towards the rectory pew.   She for her part
turns pale and red, and wonders how she shall get
through the service.   What must her old lover think of
her conduct ?   For, of course, he cannot know that her
husband had not taken note of so important a fact as the
squire's name.   She determines to make her explanation
to Miss Norman directly after church, and then, with

calm self-forgetfulness, she gives up her mind to the service. The music is a great help, and her husband's sermons always rivet her attention. She remains in her seat till every one has left the church except the organist, who continues the strain until she knows her brother will be out of hearing, for he likes to hear the music as he walks alone through the churchyard. Mrs. Chamberlayne and Miss Norman meet in the church-porch, and shake hands cordially without an introduction.

"Can you spare me a few minutes?" began Lilian. "I have a confession to make."

The children were told to take care of each other, and Lilian soon made Eleanor understand the state of the case.

"You will believe that I should never have come here had I known that Arthur was the squire. I could see by the one glance I had of him that he has not got over the trouble I gave him, and I am afraid it may be a trial to him to meet me."

She spoke with simple straightforwardness, and Eleanor was completely disarmed. She had secretly resented the conduct of her brother's love more than she admitted to herself, but now she realised the state of the case fully. She did wish that it had been otherwise, for Lilian would have been the right person in the right place at Norman-hurst, but, indeed, she was suitable to any place, and Eleanor could not but feel that Edward Chamberlayne was worthy of his wife. He would have borne such a disappointment as Arthur had drooped under with cheerful courage, and therefore he was more worthy of such a

6*

prize as he had won than Arthur would have been. The two ladies parted with mutual satisfaction, feeling as if they had known each other for years.

"I will explain the case to Arthur," Eleanor had said.

"And I will not tell my stupid old Edward, it will only make him unhappy; though, of course, he is not really to blame, and we cannot give up our charge now. I hope Arthur will find out before you get rid of us that things are really all for the best."

The simple way in which Lilian spoke of "Arthur" charmed Eleanor. He had been "Arthur" to her, and she could not change. He had been her friend, and she could not become formal because she had not been able to give him love as well as friendship.

Geoffrey was very loth to part with his new friends, but when Mrs. Chamberlayne asked if he would stay to dinner, he was too loyal to his first friend to stay without her.

Arthur came in to luncheon with his face clouded as it had not been since Geoffrey's arrival at Normanhurst. Eleanor could not find him before luncheon to give him Lilian's message. As soon as he had made a pretence of eating—for he hardly touched anything; only drank a great deal of water—he rose to leave the room.

"I must speak to you, Arthur," his sister said, with quiet decision.

"I shall be in my study," he answered, and left the room.

"Has uncle Arthur been naughty?" asked Geoffrey.

"Not quite naughty," answered Eleanor. "He had

a great trouble once, and he did not bear it well. He was impatient, and he kept on being impatient, and now I think he is going to be taught how to be patient."

Eleanor hated mysteries, and she had a theory that children were never too young to be treated as reasonable beings. Of course, it was often not advisable to tell them what the state of the case actually was; but they might always be told enough to enlist their sympathy.

Geoffrey looked full of interest now, and observed, " I can quite understand being impatient. Poor uncle Arthur ! I hope he will soon be better;" and then of his own accord the little fellow trotted off to Natalie, while Eleanor proceeded to her brother's study.

Very few words made Arthur understand what had happened, and he said, with a heavy sigh, "She could do no wrong."

Eleanor saw that this was not the time to say more, so, kissing him very tenderly, she left him to fight with his trouble by himself.

CHAPTER IX.

AMONGST THE FLOWERS.

ELEANOR wondered how Arthur would meet his old love face to face. She need not have feared. He was coldly courteous to Mr. and Mrs. Chamberlayne, receiving them because he could not help himself, as the substitutes of the rector and his wife, but merely offering the barest courtesies which their relative positions exacted.

Lilian sighed and said to herself, " Poor Arthur, how glad I am I did not marry him." She looked at her Edward, in his threadbare black, as he smiled over the squire's unwilling civilities. He was inclined to attribute his somewhat unpolished manners to what Natalie called *boompkeenism.*

Meanwhile the days glided by very happily for Geoffrey and his new friends. He found that Fée, the only daughter amongst the four children, was quite as unused to children as he was. She had been her mother's constant companion ever since she was born. As for Hugh, the available boy—for the next one, though he could walk, was happier in his perambulator—he was a boy in every sense of the word.

The three children met daily, though Geoffrey never would forego his walks and rides and drives with Eleanor, even for his new friends. Natalie was charmed with the pretty little demoiselle, and offered to give both Fée and Hugh French lessons. Mrs. Chamberlayne accepted the offer gratefully. "A Parisian accent may be most important to Fée one of these days," she said, simply. Arthur happened to hear the remark, and left the room abruptly. Of course Mrs. Chamberlayne knew how very poor they were, how everything depended on Edward's life, for her own modest fortune would hardly keep them in the merest necessaries if they were without the bread-winner.

Arthur, in the solitude of his study, was fighting over again the unwon struggle between his sorrow and his better nature.

How different it might have been! As his wife, Lilian would have been the queen of the county, their children would have enjoyed every advantage, and he would have been happy in a wife's love. He little knew how differently Lilian contemplated this case of "might have been." He could not deny that she always seemed cheerful, but he could not believe she preferred the poor present and the uncertain future to the prosperity and wealth she had rejected in her thoughtless girlhood.

Geoffrey was very proud of explaining country ways and sights and sounds to these little town-bred children. He had really quite forgotten that scarcely two months had passed since he became a country boy.

The first time the children heard the birds singing

they could hardly contain their delight. They were silent for fear of interrupting the concert, and even Geoffrey was not very familiar with the full burst of melody which welcomes April. March had been very cold, and the birds had only sung fitfully by ones and twos. Spring came upon them suddenly after several very wet days, and the birds welcomed the first day in a burst of melody. "It is delicious," Geoffrey whispered at last. "Of course you know it is the birds, but *I* have never heard so many myself all at once."

Though Arthur never accepted nor offered hospitalities in the neighbourhood, he gave a yearly entertainment to his tenants, at which Eleanor presided with him, so that, in spite of his moroseness, it was pleasant. Nothing could be dull when Miss Norman was present. Besides this he let her have as many school-feasts and village-feasts as she thought wholesome, and this year she determined to celebrate Geoffrey's birthday, which happened on the first of May, with a faithful revival of all the pretty May-day customs of olden times.

Mr. and Mrs. Chamberlayne entered heartily into the idea. The children were almost beside themselves with delight. The novelty to them of the proposed fête of course added to its attractions.

The April days lengthened, the soft showers alternated with sunshine, which grew warmer after each shower; flowers became abundant in woods and meadows, and on the last day of April everybody who could carry a basket went out a-maying in the Normanhurst woods and fields.

Geoffrey, with a scarlet face, was rushing up from one of the woods with Hugh, carrying between them a clothes-basket full of cowslips.

In the very centre of the large old-fashioned garden there was a wide expanse of smooth turf. On one side was a bower covered with honeysuckles and all kinds of sweet creepers. Some gardeners were making a framework of willows, flagstaffs marked out the ground, and a long pole near a deep hole in the middle of the space suggested the time-honoured Maypole. Eleanor and Lilian were in the honeysuckle - arbour, busily weaving wreaths of bluebells, forget-me-nots, cowslips, faint sweet cuckoo - flowers, marsh - marigolds, which really did shine like gold, if not like fire, in the shady retreat, and every sort of spring flower, which were heaped round and over them in profusion.

"My pet!" exclaimed Amie, as Geoffrey rushed headlong into the arbour, "what a flaming face ! Don't you think you had better sit down for a few minutes and tie up some bunches for Mrs. Chamberlayne and me?" Geoffrey shook his head, and was darting off again, when Mrs. Chamberlayne said, gently, "I really do want some help, please, Geoffrey."

She was covering some wire frames, composed of one circle and two half-circles crossed, which, when finished, looked like crowns of flowers. They were the old-fashioned garlands used in the fourteenth century in the royal processions, when kings and queens went out a-maying, and princesses got up at dawn to wash their faces in May dew, securing thereby enhanced beauty.

"If you will tie up the bunches for me it will help me to get on so much quicker."

Geoffrey sat down reluctantly. Hugh had already set him a good example by preparing bunches for Miss Norman, who was weaving the garlands for the Maypole. When finished it was to be an exact imitation of the famous Maypole before St. Andrew-under-Shaft.

The actual pole was gaily twisted round with pink and white calico, like the old-fashioned barbers' poles that still project from ancient establishments for hairdressing in sleepy country towns, and even in some remote streets in London. Then there were to be five garlands—one very large, suspended about the centre, and kept in its place by wires covered with flowers. Flags floated from the extreme top, then came a compact garland which formed a crown. A garland a size larger came next, then the principal garland; below this, two more graduated garlands, one smaller than the other, and the pole was to be finished off with bright flags. Little Fée came in with some particular flowers her mother had sent her for, and this reconciled Geoffrey to his sedentary occupation as she helped him to pick out the best flowers, and he really did find the cool shade and the quiet rather pleasant than otherwise. The day was exceptionally hot, Amie and Lilian were both in white gowns, and they looked very fresh and spring-like.

The outward trappings of woe expressed nothing to Eleanor's mind; she had conformed with custom so far as to wear black during the cold months, but now that spring had burst upon them with summery warmth she put on the white dresses she always wore in fine weather, but she did not wear bright ribands according to her usual custom. She could not bear to associate gloom with Marian's memory, and even Arthur smiled when she appeared in white again. Man-like, he did not care to be constantly reminded of a common sorrow, for it was only his personal grief that he cared to cherish.

He had rather favoured the proposed May-day ceremonial, anything that gave Geoffrey pleasure pleased his uncle. Arthur was slowly, almost imperceptibly, but surely, coming to a better state of mind.

Now a long procession approaches the arbour, and Geoffrey, Hugh, and Fée dart out to meet it. Some twenty children, varying in age from fourteen to eight, appear, walking two and two and carrying baskets between them well filled with flowers.

Eleanor goes to the door of the arbour and receives them with kind smiles and warm thanks, and Geoffrey and his friends inspect the contents with critical eyes. They have been trained by now to know the most lasting sort of flower, and the required length of stalk.

One little girl had brought a basket full of heads, daisy tops, as Geoffrey called them contemptuously, but Eleanor came to the rescue, for the little maiden looked tearful, and she said kindly she should find a use for them.

"They will do to scatter for me and the queen to walk upon," added Geoffrey, patronisingly. He would not have willingly hurt any one's feelings, especially at such a time, and the little heads-woman was comforted.

Luncheon caused a diversion, and the flower-pickers were also to be regaled. After luncheon Geoffrey was allowed to resume his picking labours, which were certainly more congenial than the tying duties, even with Fée's deft assistance.

The bright day brightened into a glorious rosy evening, giving delightful promise of just such another day for to-morrow. The cuckoos called to each other, causing the children great amusement. They quickly learnt to imitate the note so accurately that they quite took the elders in. Tea was brought out into the arbour for the ladies, and of course the children shared the *al fresco* repast.

"I don't think May-day will be any nicer," said little Fée, nestling close to her mother's side.

"Perhaps not as nice," was the answer.

"Oh, but it shall be as nice," said Geoffrey and Hugh in a breath ; "we will make it as nice."

"Weather being favourable," said Eleanor, "I think we may reasonably hope for a very happy day. It is a great pleasure to make a number of people happy, and I am sure, dear children, you will enjoy that pleasure as much as your own private amusement. You will think of the little village children who have not all the good things that have fallen to your lot, and for this one day you will make their pleasure yours."

"Our pleasure will be theirs," said Geoffrey ; "because we shall be enjoying the same things. Is that what you mean, Amie?"

"I mean that, and I also mean that you must do all

you can to amuse them. When the grand ceremony is over, you must play with them nicely, you must look after them at their tea, and you must see, in short, that no one is left out of the fun. I know little Fée will befriend the shy girls, and you and Hugh must do the same by the boys."

It was time to go in now; the children were to go to bed very early, and Eleanor was not long after Geoffrey. She had to be up at four the next morning, and she had the happy healthy faculty of being able to go to sleep as early as she pleased. She had been up at six that day, and even Arthur must be condemned to a solitary evening for this one occasion. "Why should you not go in to the rectory?" she suggested; and he actually acted on the suggestion, and spent a very pleasant evening with Edward Chamberlayne, whose wife had followed Eleanor's example, and had gone to bed with the birds and the children.

CHAPTER X.

MAY-DAY.

THE sun had not yet appeared, but he had sent some heralds which promised well. Little delicate pink clouds in a pale blue sky, not making morning red, or even rosy, but telling as plainly as possible that the day was going to be fine. One star after another went out as the sun's light dispensed with these little night lights.

" A sweet south wind, that meant no rain," was " the best thing under the sun," for that day, at any rate.

Eleanor was standing dressed by Geoffrey's crib on this wonderful First of May. His eyes were opening, and her pleasant smiles and warm greetings reminded him that he was six years old, and that it was the morning of the First of May.

"Many happy returns," said Amie.

"The same to you," he answered, eagerly. "And may I wash myself this morning, dear delicious Amie?"

He thought it would be a step towards manhood, and he knew his aunt could refuse him nothing on this day. In spite of his joyous anticipations he remembered that this was the first birthday which his own darling mother had not greeted, and that she never would again be able to wish him many happy returns. His father was away too, and though he might be with him on another occasion he would be away to-day. Geoffrey looked quite grave while he was washing and dressing; and Amie seemed to enter into his feelings, she talked so gravely and nicely. She did not mention his mother, but she spoke to him as that mother would have spoken had she been there; and when he was quite dressed his thoughts returned to the business in hand.

Great branches of blackthorn converted the erection of willows on which the gardeners had been occupied the day before into a May bower fit for a fairy queen and her consort. The maypole would have certainly taken the prize if any number of maypoles had appeared to compete with it. The symmetry of the wreaths, the freshness of the flowers, the harmonious blending of colour, left nothing to be desired. A little garden of primroses round the foot of this erection formed a charming finish. Two lines of flags led up to the maypole and on to the throne-room. Indeed, flags floated from every available place, and gave a most holiday appearance to everything. The sun smiled down most benignly on all the preparations and obligingly drank up the May dew before eight o'clock. Amie and Geoffrey, Mrs. Chamberlayne, Fée, Hugh, Gerald, and even baby, had washed their faces in this excellent preparation, which was warranted to improve any complexion; at least, baby's face was washed for him, and all the children crowded round eagerly to see if he had improved. "I do think his face is not quite so red," said Geoffrey, critically; "but oh,

Mrs. Chamberlayne, do you think if you rubbed some on his gums it would make his teeth grow? I saw him yawning just now, and he has not got one single tooth in his mouth. I think that is why he is so very ugly. His face is not so red as it was when he came, and his eyes open nearly as wide as Fée's doll's eyes when the wire works right; but it is a pity he should have no teeth."

"They will come in time, dear Geoffrey," said Mrs. Chamberlayne. "But I have no objection to try if May dew will hasten the operation." And she dipped her finger in the grass, which was still glistening with jewels, and suited the action to the words.

Everything was ready, the programme was written out, Geoffrey had received all his birthday presents; his father had sent him a lovely statuette amongst other things, which was so like his mother that Geoffrey cried over it.

He sent a picture of himself, for fear Geoffrey should forget what he was like, and this the boy received as a present from his mother. Indeed, it had been hers, so it was not an unnatural idea.

"I suppose she does not want it in heaven," he said, "she can see father whenever she likes. But I hope she does not like any one up there better than she likes us. Of course she loves the baby as much—that is quite right—and she likes all the angels and people, but I do hope not better."

"There is no better in heaven, darling," said Amie, with tears in her bright eyes; "it is all best."

"Amie, heaven is up yonder, isn't it?" said he, pointing

to the blue sky, and looking up with his own eyes, which seemed to have taken their colour from above, as if he would fain see into heaven itself.

His aunt said "yes," though, indeed, at that moment it seemed as if heaven was everywhere.

" Then is it hard in heaven ? " Amie looked puzzled, so Geoffrey went on, "Why don't their legs come through ? "

Eleanor would not have laughed for the world, but this very material question was almost too much for her gravity; however, she busied herself with one of the presents, and answered with scarcely a tremble in her voice,—

" They have wings you know."

" All of them ?   Babies and men and women, as well as angels ? "

" We know the children are angels because it says in the Bible of the little children, ' Their *angels* do always behold the face of my Father.' "

Geoffrey said no more, but, by the expression of his face, he was evidently satisfied.   And now it was time to dress. Uncle Arthur's present was a suit for the occasion, and Eleanor had planned a charming little dress.   The suit was of Lincoln-green velvet; a tunic and hose, and dainty shoes, with silver chain and bugle, a quiver with arrows, the most exquisite bow in the world, and a green bonnet with white plumes, turned Geoffrey into a perfect Robin Hood, according to tradition and pictures.   Hugh, as Little John, though very tall for his age, corresponded to the style a little better than his gigantic namesake

7

appears to have done. Fée, Robin's "Maid Marion," the elected queen of the day, looked charming. She was all in white, without a bit of colour, except what nature had given her. Her pink cheeks were pinker than usual, her dark eyes shone like two stars, her golden hair looked as bright as sunbeams.

Eleanor had dressed all the children ; Mrs. Chamberlayne would not deprive her of what was evidently a pleasure. She could afford it, and had Lilian been in her place she would have done the same thing with equal generosity and simplicity. In the same spirit she herself accepted the pretty white dress and the hat, both exactly like Eleanor's, and it was hard to say which lady was happiest, the giver or the receiver.

It is often quite as generous to accept as it is to offer, and even Arthur was almost cheerful on this

> Maddest, merriest day
> Of all the glad New Year.

And now the school children are arriving. The long lines of happy flower-laden, flower-decked children as they wind amongst the trees, look like moving garlands.

A rush cart, covered with flowers, is at the door. Rushes strew the bottom and are ingeniously plaited round the sides, so that the cart really looks as if it were made of rushes. This cart is drawn by a proud white ass, a garland of flowers encircles the animal's neck, and a boy in a suit of Lincoln green stands at his head and restrains his ardour. A bodyguard of boys in green, with bows and arrows, need no further label to proclaim them Robin Hood's "merrie men."

And now Amie and Lilian begin to marshal the procession. First, Jack-in-the-green moves merrily forward. Geoffrey had seen such a personage in London, but he was dingy indeed compared to the fresh ivy tower which headed this truly rural procession. The London Jack-in-the-green had always been a profound mystery until, the very year before, Geoffrey had caught sight of a pair of sturdy human legs, after which he lost all interest in the moving tower. "There is a man inside," he had said, contemptuously; "any one could do that. I thought it did itself."

But this Jack quite mystified the school-children. Geoffrey had made a great point of hiding his legs, and clever Amie had covered his very feet with leaves, so that the illusion was complete.

Next to "Jack" marched eight boys, two and two, carrying flags. Then came eight girls carrying the splendid garlands which Mrs. Chamberlayne had manufactured. They were so large that it took four girls to carry one. Two walked in front and two behind. Then came four boys carrying wands decked with flowers. Then half Robin Hood's merrie men. Little John rode an ass just in front of the cart. Robin Hood and Maid Marion bowed right and left as if they been accustomed to receive homage from their birth. Behind the cart walked the crown-bearers, the bearers of sceptres and balls, the rest of Robin Hood's merrie men, more garland, wand, and flag bearers, and the procession ended in

7 *

a long tail of school-children walking two and two. The teachers, Eleanor, Mr. Chamberlayne, and Lilian, kept the moving procession in capital order as they proceeded down the terrace singing May carols, and forming a moving garden paying a visit to the gardens that could not move to meet them. Down the carriage drive, then sharp to the right under some thick yew trees, out on to the broad terrace bright with spring flowers, past the bowling green, the famous cedars, and into the old-fashioned plaisaunce with its tortuous paths. Now the procession winds along the banks of the pretty pond, and is reproduced upside down in its clear depths. Then it disappears under some wonderful yews, but only for a minute. Jack-in-the-green stands out a bright spot on the dark background of yews, and the brighter company gradually emerge. The cuckoo tries to drown the children's carol, the birds only attempt to join in the chorus, with charming effect.

At last the procession reaches the green space where stands the Maypole. The singers pause, the village band, hidden behind the trees, strikes up, " God save the Queen." Uncle Arthur himself lifts Robin Hood and Maid Marion out of the state coach; the children form two lines and scatter flowers at the feet of the royal outlaw and his queen, and the pair are soon seated in the throne-room. Robin unbonnets his head, and the royal diadem of marsh-marigolds is well set off by his bright golden brown curls. Fée has already been crowned appropriately with lilies-of-the-valley and forget-me-nots ; and the tiny sceptres of flowers and balls of cowslip heads are very sweet illustrations of the usual insignia of royalty.

Then every one does homage. Uncle Arthur kneels down with such courtly grace that Natalie wonders how she ever dared think him a "boompkeen." Amie always does everything well; and Lilian says she is not the first mother who has acknowledged her daughter as her Sovereign Lady and Queen, and she kisses the little dimpled hand as respectfully as if she were one of the village children. "Kings always kiss their lady subjects," said Geoffrey, as Lilian was about to kiss his hand. He stept down from his flowery throne as he spoke and gallantly kissed Mrs. Chamberlayne on the cheek.

When the reception was over, king, queen, merrie men, children, and teachers all joined hands round the Maypole. There were so many that they had to form three circles, one inside the other. They danced until they rolled down on the grass from exhaustion: even the elders had some trouble in keeping their feet.

At last the procession reformed, and returned to the house. The tables were amply spread on the lawns, and the serious business of the day commenced.

"My goodness, Amie, I did not think anybody could eat so much," observed Geoffrey, as he panted under the burden of a platter of buns. "One boy cried because he could not eat another of these buns. He had eaten four already, a whole plate of bread and butter, and two wedges of cake. I told him to stand up, but he said he had tried that, and then I offered him some tea, but he had drunk six mugs full already. He says he is the prize eater, and I quite believe him."

" Oh, Johnny, Johnny," said Eleanor, approaching the prize eater, " I am sorry to hear that you are as greedy as ever."

Johnny rubbed his knuckles up and down his face, which was so fat and firm that he could hardly make an impression even on the cheeks.

At last the tea was over, and the children set to work to play with the utmost gravity. It was wonderful how even the prize eater managed to run, to duck in water for apples, and to rummage in flour for a sixpence. The only thing he could not manage was a sack; he could not rise the least bit in the world, but fell heavily as soon as he was let go, and did not even try to get up again.

Neither Geoffrey nor the Chamberlayne children had ever seen jumping in sacks before, and the two boys insisted on trying their 'prentice powers. Very well they did it too, after a first failure. Geoffrey had so much spring in him that he went along like an indiarubber ball, and actually bounced up again when he did fall. Then they had wheel-barrow races, the drivers being blindfolded, and the results were very funny. Then boys made themselves into wheel-barrows, running on their hands, while another boy held their legs and drove them.

The girls played at " threading my needle," and all the mysterious games to which the gentler sex is con. demned. Amie preferred the boys, but, whatever Lilian and Fée felt on the subject, they devoted their energies to the girls, and everybody went away perfectly contented and happy. There had not been "a drop of rain the whole of the live-long day;" and Geoffrey, on being asked what he had left to wish for when the day was over, promptly replied,—

"To have it all over again."

CHAPTER XI.

A LITTLE MERMAN.

ELEANOR hardly echoed Geoffrey's wish. She was thoroughly tired, but she only laughed as she wished him good-night, and told him to enjoy it all over again in a dream.

"I hope you will not be overdone," she said, as she kissed Lilian, and wrapped a shawl round her shoulders, in case the evening of such a day should be damp.

"No fear," was the cheerful answer; "I am never overdone when I am happy. And I have been very happy to-day."

She had been happy for many reasons. Of course, like all good mothers, she rejoiced in her children's joy. Then, like all kindly hearted women, she was glad to see other people, and especially children, glad. She liked to see a person in Eleanor's position doing her duty so thoroughly and joyously. Her husband, being part of herself, entered entirely into all these feelings. But there was one joy that she shared with no one, and yet which concerned every one.

Arthur Norman had treated her for the first time as a friend, in a simple, natural manner. It might have been

only due to the general hilarity, which brought forget-
fulness of self to the most egotistic nature ; but it was a
good beginning, and it would be difficult to go back to
stiffness with such a genial person as Mrs. Chamberlayne.

Arthur began to own to himself that it was very pleasant to see so many people happy, and to forget his
carefully cherished sorrow, with the cause of it actually
before his eyes ; so that everybody went to bed that
night the better for the past day.

" May glides onward into June." Its course was very
even. The children became faster friends than ever,
and did each other great good. Geoffrey and Natalie
had no time for differences ; he was glad enough to get
through his lessons, which were really no trouble to him,
and he was never now condemned to spend his hours
of recreation or to take his walks abroad alone with his
bonne.

As for Eleanor, the society of Mr. Chamberlayne and
Lilian was quite a new experience to her ; or rather it
revived old experiences, for the dear uncle and aunt, now
no more, had loved to gather pleasant people round them,
and their house had been considered the pleasantest in
the country.

Arthur, in spite of himself, enjoyed the society of a
cultivated man. " Depend upon it, Amie," said Lilian
(she and her children had all adopted Geoffrey's
pretty pet name for Eleanor), " the melody of a child's
voice, the charms of that boy's nature, are acting on
Arthur as David's harp acted on Saul. The evil spirit is
being exorcised, and it will not return in this case.

When once Arthur's better nature asserts the superiority, he will never give way again.   Next winter you will have the house full; you will be the patroness of the great county ball; there will be a mistress of Normanhurst who will be called Mrs., and not Miss Norman, while some other stately home will be blessed to call Eleanor its queen."

Eleanor shook her head, while she laughed.   She was quite contented with things as they were, but was too young and too bright-natured not to enjoy social inter-course thoroughly.

The roses, for which Normanhurst is famous, are in their glory.   June has given place to July.   " June rose, by May dew impearled," had become roses in abundance, brought to perfection by June sunshine.

It was so intensely hot that even Eleanor indulged in the *dolce far niente*, and was compelled to lie still during the lagging hours of the burning noontide, under the trees near the water.   Lilian would sit beside her, with her baby, an excellent child who never cried ; and they talked whenever, as Eleanor said, there was air enough to carry sound from one to the other.

Only the children were irrepressible.   They ran about unceasingly, and though it must be admitted their com-plexions were not improved by exposure and exertion, they did not seem to suffer in any other way.

Luncheon has been over for some hours, Geoffrey and Hugh have been playing cricket until even they are willing to own that it is hot.   Fée has actually deserted the boys to listen to a story which Natalie is telling her. They are a little contemptuous, but too polite to interfere.

"Let us go and look how the gold fish are liking the heat," said Geoffrey, and off the restless couple set. There was a little garden through a labyrinth that was the delight of the children. In the first place Natalie had never mastered the mysteries of the approach, so she could never follow them into this retreat. Then it was so wonderfully beautiful — "like fairyland," the little fairy-named sister would say.

Here the three children played at being other people ; no one ever disturbed them, for if Lilian and Eleanor ever followed them they availed themselves of the mazes of the labyrinth and watched and listened, unseen themselves. The garden itself was full of roses, and in the middle there was a broad shallow stone basin devoted to gold-fish. A slender jet of water played continuously. A little stone boy without any clothes on supported the vase from which the water rose. Broad water-lily leaves sheltered the gold-fish, and dragon-flies hovered over the white flowers, looking like humming-birds. Indeed, the whole scene was suggestive of the tropics in miniature. Everything was so luxuriant, the heat was so intense, the sky was so blue, the air was so still, it was difficult to believe in active life and moving human beings. Even the very active boys were awed into stillness, and sat on the edge of the stone basin watching the gold-fish and the dragon-flies, and saying nothing.

Geoffrey had a little stick in his hand, which he

kept dipping into the water, thereby startling the fish from their fancied security, and causing them to exert themselves most unnecessarily on this hot day. Presently an idea struck Geoffrey. He dipped the stick into the water, and found that it only came up to the top, while the stick did not reach up to his own waist.

"I have a good mind to have a dip," he said at last. Hugh's eyes sparkled, but Geoffrey continued in a fatherly manner, after feeling him critically, "You are too hot; besides, your mother might object. I must just ask my buttons if Amie has ever forbidden me to do anything of the sort."

Every time Eleanor prohibited anything Geoffrey made a note by means of a button.

"Button one, not to slide down the balusters. Oh, that was a pity, Hugh; I could slide splendidly! Button two, not to go near the big ponds or the river by myself. Nothing about any of the fountains, and nothing about this bath," he added, after doing every button conscientiously, even those that secured his knickerbockers at the knee.

He forgot how hot he was himself when he criticised Hugh's state, and prepared to divest himself of his garments. Hugh watched him wistfully, but he was younger, and he felt that Geoffrey knew best. Besides he was not very fond of cold water. Eleanor had quite educated Geoffrey to the taste, and he looked forward to his daily cold bath with genuine pleasure.

"I think Amie will be rather pleased with me for taking a cold bath," he said, complacently, as he wriggled out of his shirt and sat down on the edge of the basin to take off his boots and stockings. In another minute he had let himself slide into the water. It was rather deeper than he had expected, and the first shock was certainly severe. He had come to the dangerous stage of heat, for while the boys had been sitting silently they had cooled imperceptibly. It is more dangerous at this stage to undergo a shock either from cold water or cold air than in the extreme state of heat, which is the immediate result of violent exertion.

The water was nearly up to his shoulders, and the fish seemed much disturbed as his little gleaming form appeared amongst them. The dragon-flies only changed flowers, and watched him superciliously from a respectful distance.

After the first shock, however, Geoffrey made himself quite at home, and kept assuring Hugh that it was delicious, though his teeth chattered a little still. He helped himself along by the strong stems of the water-lilies, and with his arm round the stone boy, to let the water come down on his head from the fountain.

He made such a pretty picture that Hugh was struck by the effect, as he called out, "How jolly you look!"

Little Fée, dancing into the garden at this moment, exclaimed, "Are you playing at Adam? Oh, let me be Eve!"

But Eleanor and Lilian were behind, and came into the garden in time to prevent this representation of Paradise.

"Geoffrey!" exclaimed Amie.

"Oh, my dear," he answered, "it is jollier than jolly !
Will you come in too? I was sure there was no harm,
because I measured with a stick to see if it was as deep
as me, and I found it was all right; and I know you like
me to have a cold bath. I did not let Hugh come in;
he is not so tall as I am, and he has not been so used
to the country; and he was very obedient. It is
delicious."

Amie was in such rapt admiration of the effect as a
picture that she stood looking and looking, until Lilian,
with a stronger maternal instinct, suggested that, as he
had probably been very hot before he got into the water,
he might be running a risk of getting a chill.

Arthur and Mr. Chamberlayne appeared on the scene
most unexpectedly, and were very much amused. Uncle
Arthur proposed to catch this whale that was disturbing
his minnows, and Geoffrey, quite entering into the fun of
the thing, slid down from his throne, and, gliding in and
out of the leaves and lilies, kept biting at the stick his
uncle held out, but never swallowing the bait. Lilian
had hastened up to the house for a bath-towel, for she
had felt uneasy about the boy. Her own Hugh was still
in such a state of heat that she was sure Geoffrey was
not likely to have been much cooler when he turned
himself, as her daughter had suggested, into a little
Adam.

"Now, Arthur," she said, "display your piscatorial
skill and catch the fish."

She had never called him Arthur since they had met
on these altered terms, but it had come out now so natu-

rally that her husband did not notice it, and Arthur himself felt quite grateful to her for this sisterly treatment. She did not take Marian's place, but she seemed to fill up a void at Normanhurst that Marian's marriage had left vacant. As for Eleanor, she loved her already as if she had been her sister indeed, and Mr. Chamberlayne was quite as great an acquisition in his way.

Meanwhile, Geoffrey was drawn out of the basin, obedient but reluctant; and he looked so lovely, with the water dripping from every part of him, and making his shining curly hair brighter and more curly, that even matter-of-fact Arthur was loth to hide his beauty in the great towel. However, Lilian was firm, and he was rolled up like a mummy, and carried into the house.

Eleanor picked up his clothes, and followed with Mr. Chamberlayne, laughing heartily over her pet's escapade.

Lilian looked grave and preoccupied, and, though Geoffrey seemed all right after he was dressed, he could not eat his tea, and towards evening his eyes began to look unnaturally bright, and his hand felt very hot and burning when she took it in hers as he wished her goodnight.

When Amie came up to bed he was tossing from side to side in his little crib, talking incoherently, with his pulse galloping and his cheeks burning. The doctor looked very grave, and Arthur was beside himself with anxiety. Eleanor, as usual, controlled her own feelings, and proved herself worthy of her sister's trust.

She was too purposeful to waste her thoughts on useless regrets. No one was to blame; accidents will happen in spite of every precaution.

Lilian came up to help; everything was done that could be done ; and these two good women knew that the issue was in wise and safe hands.

It would indeed be well if all mothers and guardians could learn the blessed lesson of self-control. It is one that should be instilled early, and example teaches the lesson much better than precept. Lilian and Eleanor had both been well brought-up in this respect.

CHAPTER XII.

ILLNESS.

ARTHUR telegraphed to London for the most eminent
doctors, and on their arrival they looked as grave as their
country brother. They said the child had evidently a
fine constitution, which might pull him through if the
fever could be subdued. On the other hand, his
strength and being struck down suddenly in full health
would add intensity to the course of the fever, which
would continue to rise for some days, after which they
would again consult; Mr. Howard, the Normanhurst
doctor, would treat him rightly in the meanwhile.
Indeed, there was very little to do except to watch
him most carefully.

Arthur, after hearing the verdict, set off for Italy.
No one could bear to think of Mr. Gordon receiving
such a telegram as they must send to summon him, and
then hurrying home alone to find—ah, what? Arthur
would be able to find him and bring him to Normanhurst, at least before the crisis should be over. It would
be a relief to be doing something in the meanwhile.
Mr. Gordon's head-quarters were at Rome, and by great
good-fortune he was busy in his studio when Arthur

8

reached the immortal city. He was on the eve of setting off on a fortnight's expedition with a friend, and would have left no address, as they meant to go wherever their fancy led, and to linger, equally according to fancy.

The man who had practised entire resignation when called upon to give up the wife who had indeed made earth a paradise for him during seven happy years, did not give way now when he heard of his son's danger. He hid his face for a few minutes, but he was actually smiling when he looked up. It was not indeed the smile that usually illumines the faces of men and women, it was such a smile that communion with the Unseen, yet ever Present, alone could call up on a living face.

Arthur did not even for a moment think that Geoffrey Gordon was wanting in deep feeling when he brought him the news of his little Geoffrey's illness.

He only felt fully for the first time how ill he had borne his own trouble, and he determined that, whatever might be the issue of this new sorrow, which would affect him most deeply, he would never again give way to gloom or moroseness.

Mr. Gordon made all arrangements for his immediate departure and his future return. "Whatever happens, Arthur, will be best, and in any case I shall return. I must finish this." He drew back a heavy velvet curtain, and even at this early stage the sculptured effigy of Marian almost seemed to breathe.

"There may be something to add to the group," said Geoffrey, with so bright a smile that Arthur could not trust himself to meet its full radiance, but knelt down and hid his face against the white marble.

Poor little Geoffrey was tossing about, rarely conscious, and indeed consciousness was not to be desired. His sufferings seemed too intense when he realised them.

Lilian could hardly bear to be in the room then, and even the practised nurse turned away, especially when the brave little fellow tried to smile. Only Eleanor could return those smiles, "scarce of earth, nor all divine." She was always bright and brave and helpful, her voice never faltered, she never seemed weary, and her hand alone could raise him without pain.

The doctor said the bright curls must be shaved off. Ice did not afford the least relief, and, indeed, the hair was so thick that the head could not feel the full benefit of the applications. Eleanor took the scissors and began clipping the little glittering rings which clustered round his head so closely and so prettily.

"Mother's curls," he murmured. "If I have got to go to heaven without them she will miss them, even if she knows me without them. Will you bury them in the little box with me, Amie?"

"No, my precious one," she answered, brightly, "I will show them to you years hence, please God. I will take great care of them."

Lilian and the nurse, and even Mr. Chamberlayne, who happened to be paying his daily visit, fairly broke down, but Eleanor smiled as she continued, "There, I think you will feel the ice better now, and perhaps we

8 *

shall not have to shave your dear head entirely. Father would not know you perhaps without any hair."

A little curl had fallen on his breast, he put his finger through it, and said very sadly,—

"I wasn't naughty, Amie, was I, to get into the foun-ain? I counted all my buttons, and I couldn't find anything about it; and besides you all laughed, except Hugh's and Fée's mother. Why did not Fée's mother laugh?"

"You were not at all naughty, my pet, but we were foolish and thoughtless. Fée's mother looked grave because she thought that it was dangerous to get into cold water when you were hot."

"I must put that on my buttons if I get well," he said, with a sigh, and then he began to ramble. "I don't want to go to heaven. I am quite happy enough. I will bear all the pain if I may only get well. I should like to go to heaven some day, but it is such a little short time to see the earth, only six years and two months."

Eleanor was still applying the ice, but at these words her hand trembled for the first time since the boy had been taken ill, her eyes filled with tears and she turned deadly pale.

He was quiet after this for a little, and the ice seemed to relieve him. Mr. Howard said the head need not be shaved at present, and Eleanor gathered up the beautiful curls and gave one to Lilian as she left the room to take her needful rest.

Mr. Gordon and Arthur arrived when the fever was

at its height. Geoffrey took no notice of them, but rambled on, now about May-day, then about the bath in the fountain, the Chamberlayne children, Amie, and even Natalie.

" I will never water you again, Natalie, if only I can get well," he used to say again and again, as if there was a strong connection in his mind between that feat and his present illness. " I might have given you a fever then, because you are not so used to water as I am. It would not have done me any harm to be watered. Am I a flower? Will the reaper Amie sings about gather me? Oh, don't let him cut me with a scythe like the gardeners do the grass! It would hurt me. I am a little boy, not grass, not a bud. Mother has got baby; she said before she went to heaven she left me for father."

Even Mr. Gordon's endurance was not proof against this. He had to leave the room. Only Eleanor was still brave enough to stay. She used to cry quietly. He never noticed anything going on around him now, so that as long as she could do what was necessary her quiet tears could not harm him.

At last the day of the expected crisis arrived. He was never violent even at the worst, but his sufferings from heat, and pain in his head and limbs were sad to witness. The glorious July weather was mocking those who had enjoyed it when all was well. A wet day would have been truly welcome to all those anxious watchers.

The London doctors had arrived. Every door and window was open, but scarcely a breath stirred. Some were pale and some were flushed; kind old Mr. Howard had to wipe a very suspicious mist from his spectacles every other minute. "It is the heat," he whispered to one of the great physicians, who was obliged to use his pocket-handkerchief even . more frequently than Mr. Howard; moreover, he had not the excuse of wiping his spectacles.

Poor little Geoffrey was almost unconscious from intensity of suffering.

"It is cruel to wish to keep him," says his father, as . he tries to cool the parched lips with the blessed ice, which does indeed afford relief for a moment.

The little voice is audible and coherent for the first time that day. "Mother, you have got baby, and you have got heaven. They will have nothing left if you take me from them. Oh! it makes me so hot trying to stay. It would be easier to come, but let me stay, please let me stay." And the weak hands struggled with the air, until Eleanor folded them in hers and whispered, "Darling, mother will not take you if it is best for you to stay."

He turned and looked at her, the unnatural excitement was passing away, the fever-distended pupils shrank to their natural size; then he turned those eyes, already dimming even with their old expression restored, towards his father; his own smile brightened his face; sweet and yet almost roguish.

"I don't think she will be so cruel as to take me," he murmured. The white lids with their long dark fringes fell, and with his head on his father's breast, and his hands closely locked round Eleanor's, he fell asleep.

No one dared move, everything depended on the awakening. The regular breaths, drawn so faintly that it was almost impossible to hear them, gave hope, and enabled the two who loved him best to bear the positions they were in without pain. The great London doctor held a cordial ready to give him as soon as he should move; but the sleep lasted for several hours beyond their utmost hopes.

The faint breathing strengthened imperceptibly, the fever flush faded until it left the cheek like a nautilus shell, as pure, as pale, as colourless. The long summer's day drew to a close. The curfew-bell would have tolled the knell of departing day—for it was still tolled in that old-fashioned neighbourhood—only Mr. Chamberlayne had bade the ringers stay their hands.

But in the church a goodly gathering of men and women and children knelt down to join their prayers to the good pastor's for the little life now hanging on a thread, and the choir sang with trembling voices but earnest hearts the words of the lovely evening hymn,—

> At even, ere the sun was set,
> The sick, O Lord, around Thee lay;
> Oh with what divers pains they met,
> Oh with what joy they went away.

Just as the concluding strain must have died away the long-expected awakening came.

Geoffrey drew a long deep breath and opened his eyes. "He will do now," said the great doctor. He held the glass to the boy's lips, who swallowed the cordial without a word; his father laid his head gently down on the pillow, Eleanor withdrew her hands from his relaxed hold, and every one left him to the care of the skilful tender nurse. "He will sleep till morning," was the verdict. "We shall see him during the night, and before we start to-morrow; but Mr. Howard would have done all that we have done. Careful nursing, a splendid constitution, and God's providence have been on our side."

Eleanor, who had borne up so bravely until this moment, suddenly fainted, and would have fallen if her grateful brother-in-law had not fortunately had his arm round her, while they listened to this reassuring verdict.

"Joy never kills," said Mr. Howard, as he helped Mr. Gordon to lay her down on a sofa.

In a few minutes she opened her eyes, meekly drank something that was held to her lips, asking in a dreamy voice if there was plenty for Geoffrey, and then followed his present example by falling fast asleep.

Mr. Chamberlayne was still in the church, though the congregation had dispersed. He was praying within the altar rails, feeling that prayers offered there were fraught with a special sanctity. His wife, Arthur, Mr. Gordon, and one or two others had made their way to the church and knelt down in front of the altar rails. A look from Lilian told him all was well, and he offered up a short thanksgiving that seemed to express the feelings of all.

"We shall have you back now, mother," said Hugh, as she hung over his crib, and told him the glad news; but little Fée said, "Thank God, mother, for saving Geoffrey for us, and for making you so useful to them all when he was ill."

CHAPTER XIII.

OUT OF DANGER.

ALL through the short summer's night, long after daylight had set in, with equal brightness to what had gone before but with something less of sultriness, Geoffrey slept on.

The household, worn-out with anxiety, slept late, under the reaction of merciful blessed relief. Eleanor was the first to wake and glide with noiseless footsteps into the carefully darkened room.

The nurse, with her shaded light, was reading, wakeful and watchful, and apparently quite unwearied in spite of her long vigil.

" I think he is waking," she whispered, " I will go for the doctors. He has had a beautiful sleep."

Geoffrey's eyes were wide open. There was still a look of pain in their expression, which was natural after all he had gone through ; but the unnatural brightness had quite gone, and, though he looked very pale and shadowy, he looked like Geoffrey in spite of everything.

The fever-strength had left him, and he spoke in such a feeble voice that Eleanor started, but quickly recovered herself and leant over him to catch what he was saying.

"Amie dear, do you think mother will think I did not love her?" And then with an awe-struck whisper, "And will God think I did not care for Him and heaven because I begged to stay here? I am going to stay, I am sure, now. I seemed to have my choice, and I chose to stay. You have only me for quite your own, and there are so many in heaven."

"It is all right, my darling," said Eleanor; "whatever happens is sure to be well, sure to be best."

And then the doctors came in, and the London doctors made over their charge to Mr. Howard, only recommending the greatest care. "There is a tendency to rheumatism; he must be quite a hothouse plant this winter, and then foreign parts after Christmas — heat first, afterwards German baths. By next summer we trust he may be equal to another bath in the fountain, but we hope he will not take it."

Geoffrey held out his small hand, which the doctors took, and the elder of the two did not offend his dignity as he stooped down and kissed him.

"That boy will grow up to be a remarkable man if he is spared," he said to his friend and coadjutor as they left the room. Breakfast was quite a merry meal. Mr. Norman exerted himself, and astonished Eleanor by his pleasant talk and cheerful manner.

Mr. Gordon's quiet thankfulness was less apparent; he was always patient, and though he had never given way, his manner had been intensely quiet and subdued ever since his wife's death. At the same time under all circumstances he took his part in social duties, so that his agreeable conversation seemed more a matter-of-course.

"You must not be alarmed if Geoffrey does not gain strength quickly. Mr. Howard thoroughly understands the case; if his progress seems too slow I will pay another visit in the autumn. You must not be impatient. I rather expect that his limbs may be affected. The great pain he suffered will probably take its revenge in that way. Indeed, it will be nature asserting herself and claiming repose. Don't let him try to walk if it is painful. Rest will be the best cure. He must be rubbed constantly, and I should recommend a professional rubber. However, you must wait a little till he is stronger." These were the elder doctor's parting words. He had really done nothing, as he said himself; nature had done the chief part, and careful nursing the rest. But Eleanor never could divest herself of the idea that he had saved the life of this darling of so many hearts. His kind manner, his cheerful words, his remedies even, might have done more than he allowed to be the case, and most true it is that manner is a great addition to a doctor's substantial qualifications. The sympathy born of a good heart and nature will induce strenuous efforts. Cheerfulness will keep despair at bay, kind encouraging words need not raise false hopes, and after all while there is life there is hope.

Geoffrey had noticed things more than any one fancied, and this doctor had made a great impression on him.

"He is so wise and so kind," he said, after he had gone. "I should like to be ill enough, if I must be ill, to want him again. I am sure he will cure me when it is time to cure me."

The weather began to get cooler as the long August days gave place to September. Geoffrey was slowly getting better, all but his legs. "Stupid things," he said, "they feel like a pair of tongs. At least they don't feel at all except when I try to move them."

It was now time to begin to rub, and then he felt the offending legs more than he cared for. They used to ache and prick like funny-bones, but these were signs of returning circulation, so that he tried to bear his troubles patiently.

The day came when uncle Arthur carried him into Eleanor's sitting-room for the first time. His father had returned to Italy to finish his work, and though Geoffrey was very sorry to part with him, he said that he luckily had so many friends he should not miss him as much as if he had only him to care for. He told his father this with childish candour, and with some notion of re-assuring him, for when the time came for parting Mr. Gordon's usual self-possession seemed to desert him.

"I shall come to you after Christmas, father, so it really is not long." And then the father smiled at the idea of months being anything but long to a child's mind.

Geoffrey seemed to guess his thoughts, for he said, "Months really seem short to me. It does not seem long since the winter, and I was so happy, especially after the children came to the rectory. Then I hardly ever had to be alone with Natalie. Poor Natalie, she is very kind now."

Illness had certainly not affected Geoffrey's conversational powers, and he bore the inaction of illness wonderfully well. His powers of observation developed, and he used to amuse himself with making inanimate objects talk to him. Eleanor fed the birds at her sitting-room window, and their speech soon became quite familiar to him. His aunt's sitting-room, and all its pretty arrangements, was a daily study. The other rooms in the house were most artistically arranged, but this room would have outraged the feelings of the dictators of the art-school. At the same time every true artist recognised the perfect taste which had arranged it, and the harmonious discords which made the whole charming. It was an odd-shaped room, part of it was in the thickness of the wall, it was in the oldest part of the house, and had a private staircase to itself, of the blackest oak, which led up to Eleanor's bedroom. Its corners made it more roomy that it looked, it was the cosiest room in the house, and still a good many people could gather round the fire quite comfortably. It was a warm room, and wood was always sufficient to keep up the fire. The walls were covered with pictures. Marian, Eleanor, and Arthur, as children, smiled down upon Geoffrey, and told him lots of stories. Then there were pictures of the three after they had grown up; there were beautiful sketches of the place and neighbourhood by his father; there was old China on brackets, and a mirror over the chimney, which reproduced the best part of the room in miniature, and was in itself a fairy tale to Geoffrey. All the presents Eleanor had ever received found a place here; book-cases lined one corner, and Arthur could often find a book in these shelves that was not in the grand library. There was a cottage pianoforte and an Irish harp. The latter was Geoffrey's prime delight, Eleanor was teaching him to play upon it, for it was light and could stand on his invalid table. He had a great taste for music, and his aunt's playing used to help the days to pass away; for in spite of his cheerfulness and content, the forced inaction must have been very trying to the active high-spirited boy, and though he never complained, he used to sigh a little wearily sometimes.

Then Amie's brightness acted most beneficially. She never seemed to notice the sigh, but something very amusing would suddenly strike her, and with a cheery laugh she related an anecdote that quite roused Geoffrey from what after all were rare fits of despondency.

There was an aviary and a small greenhouse combined adjoining Amie's sitting-room, and all sorts of rare birds from Africa, India, and Australia, furnished Geoffrey with never-failing interest. Arthur was always making additions to this collection, at one time it had been the only thing that in the least interested him.

Now, as it gave pleasure to Geoffrey, his uncle took more pleasure than ever in finding new sorts of birds. One day he brought back a pair of chestnut-breasted finches, very rare Australian birds, which Mr. Gould had figured very successfully in his exquisite monographs of birds of Australia, though in the letter-press he remarked that he had never had the good-fortune to see them in a state of nature. Their exceeding rarity, of course, made

Arthur appreciate them doubly as a collector and as an ornithologist. Geoffrey, after the first excitement, took little interest in the strangers, they seemed so hopelessly wild. But it was very different with a pair of African mannikins, which arrived at the same time. These little fellows, about as long as Eleanor's thumb, were most amusing. A small pagoda-shaped cage was provided for them, and they stood on a tripod table close to the head of Geoffrey's couch. They were like little crows in shape, with bills like finches. Their coats, black and glossy, would have done credit to Mr. Poole, their fit was so faultless. Their white breasts carried out the idea of a gentleman's evening suit in a spotless expanse of waist-coat. They wore black ties—Geoffrey was always telling them white ties were the proper thing with an evening dress, but they seemed to consider their fashion the best, for they did not act on their friend's suggestion. They were very tame, and did not seem to consider their position at all confining. Their little chattering voices never seemed to tire Geoffrey, who very soon established a perfect understanding with these African strangers.

Of course, the daily visits Fée and Hugh paid him were his great relaxations, and he used thoroughly to enjoy listening to them while they took their French lesson from Natalie. Their accent, though more promising than uncle Arthur's, was still far from doing credit to Natalie's Parisian French.

Geoffrey really spoke like a native, he had a remarkably good ear, and, besides, Natalie had been with him ever since he had been able to run alone.

No one grudged the little invalid any amusement, and he was naturally too well-bred to laugh rudely.

"You really are improving, Hugh," he said one day; "but you say 'pongdong,' just like uncle Arthur, instead of 'pendant' (sometimes). And I wish you would say 'tois' instead 'fwo.' Open your teeth. Fée does it better."

Natalie was much gratified by her first pupil's accuracy, and amused at the way in which he imitated the faulty as well as the correct pronunciation.

Thus September gave place to October, and autumnal gloom outside made indoor confinement less distasteful to Geoffrey. Besides, he was getting used to it, and his progress was quite satisfactory. He could walk now from his room to Amie's sitting-room; and the London doctor, who had come down on a visit to enjoy a short well-earned holiday, and to help uncle Arthur to shoot his partridges and pheasants, was surprised to find how well he had got on.

"He will be quite fit to join his father in January." And Eleanor stifled a little sigh, for it was a great sacrifice leaving home and all her pleasant duties for an indefinite time.

Of course she could not let her pet go without his faithful Amie, and no one ever knew that the expedition was not an unalloyed delight to her.

Geoffrey's mannikins wiled away November and December in the most delightful way by telling him the story of their little lives, and Eleanor wrote it down at Geoffrey's dictation.

CHAPTER XIV.

THE BIRD'S STORY.

IT was a wild wet day towards the end of October. Dead leaves were whirled against the window by the driving wind, which made such strange noises in that old rambling house that Geoffrey's birds clung to the bars of their cage and peeped out on the strange dreary scene with wonder not unmixed with awe. In spite of the weather, Eleanor had gone out to attend to a sick person; the Chamberlayne children had all got colds, and were not likely to be let out under such circumstances. Uncle Arthur and Mr. Chamberlayne were shut up in the library near a beautiful fire, enjoying a really learned discussion. They were both clever men, and had each of them received an excellent education, by which they had benefited, though Arthur had neglected his French. Under their present circumstances they were in a fair way to forget time, dinner, and even Geoffrey, who was generally first in his uncle's mind.

One of the boy's rare sighs escaped him. There was no one by to hear, and it relieved him. He felt better for it, and his eyes fell on one of his favourite mannikins, clinging with bill and claws to the wires of the cage. It

9

was looking at him so wisely that a sudden idea struck Geoffrey. "It shall tell me its story," he thought, and he prepared to listen to a fantastic tale of African life and African ways, as lived by these quaint little Negro-birds.

"The first thing I can remember is liberty," began the hen bird. She seemed to have obtained all the advantages for which her sex among human beings is now struggling. She ruled the small kingdom of the cage, took her bath and her meals in an imperious way first, and sometimes kept her husband from enjoying his by various little teasing tricks: pecking his foot when he was swallowing his drop of liquor, which evidently sent it down the wrong way; getting in front of him when he was selecting an agreeable morsel; and as for his ablutions, more than once she had made him overdo them, and very nearly drowned him. Of course, the present privilege of the whole feminine race was hers pre-eminently. She engrossed the conversation, led up to a subject, sustained it, dropped it, and did not attempt to listen to any little remarks Mr. Mannikin put in.

So she began,—

"The first thing I remember is liberty." She pecked viciously at the bar to which she was clinging. "True, I could not use my liberty, for I had no glossy black feathers, and my wings were folded very closely, my legs were curled up, and I was fitted, like those curious bits of wood you put together sometimes" (that is my joining map, thought Geoffrey), "close into the side of a creature like myself. We were in our nest, which had been our birthplace. A little mother, not nearly so large as I am now, nor so well plumaged—for from my birth I was considered a remarkable specimen for size, and, when my feathers grew, they were allowed to be unrivalled—but still this mother was not unlike me, and she was very good to my companion and to myself. During the short darkness, so different to the long black hours here, she used to spread her wings over our nest, and we used to nestle up into her white breast. During the bright sunny hours of the day she used to go with a companion, as like herself as my companion was like me, in search of food. This companion used usually to attend to my neighbour, while my mother used to drop a delicious preparation into my mouth. It was juicy and refreshing, very unlike this." The bird had hopped into the seed-box, and was discontentedly eating a grain of millet-seed.

"Was it fruit?" asked Geoffrey, eagerly. "We have plenty."

"It was delicious," answered the bird; "I do not imagine you have anything nice. While our parents were in quest of food, I used to enjoy the first taste of liberty. True, as I said before, I could not yet leave the nest, but as I got stronger each day I used to be mistress of the nest, I used to try each part, until I had decided on the most comfortable corner. Instead of wires over our heads, we had blue soft sky. I used to watch my parents as they flew through this lovely blue, and I used to long for the day when I could fly as far, perhaps farther. They never seemed to approach a brilliant

9 *

object, which I confess I could not look at without being dazzled; but I determined, when my wings would support me, to make straight for the sun. The lesser and smaller lights of the night were well enough, but they went out when the sun appeared; and therefore I thought if I reached one of the stars, or even the moon, and settled myself there, I should only have such a short time to be seen, as these could not be seen for so many hours. True, the sun used to disappear for the very few hours during which the stars shone, but he evidently went elsewhere. He used to get larger and larger as he got lower and lower in the splendid sky; and he evidently rolled over the bank of clouds on which he rested the last thing in the evening, and gave his light elsewhere. Perhaps he comes here, but he certainly does not look as bright, or stay nearly as long. At last I stood on the edge of my nest; my mother gave me a little push. She had never taken such a liberty before, and I was inclined to resent, and perhaps to return it. But I found the push was only a friendly hint, to show me what I could do. I stretched out my wings, hitherto so closely folded, to steady myself; I found they could support me! Oh, happy moment! I was cleaving the air as I had seen my parents do. Of course I could not attempt my journey to the sun on this first day of trying my wings. I was soon .tired, and glad enough to drop into the nest, though I was already beginning to despise my humble birthplace.

"What wonderful things there were to see! After one or two attempts I gave up all thoughts of visiting the sun. He was much pleasanter at a distance. Moreover, he had a good deal to do with all the lovely flowers, all the delicious fruits which made my native land so beautiful. It was owing to his light and heat that the flowers expanded and that the fruit ripened, but there was no reason to suppose that such things existed on his dazzling surface. Indeed, a wise old monkey, with a lovely blue face, something the colour of the sky at night, told me if I got to the sun I should be burnt up. I quite believed him, for I used to feel parched sometimes flying from one tree to another if the space happened to be clear. I soon learned to try and keep the luxuriant foliage of those tropical forests between myself and the sun. Poor little English boy! You do not know what beauty is. If you could have seen the birds, of every size and colour, which made my forest such a lovely spot, you could never be content in this little dingy room again. I have heard your visitors, not always, I must admit, so dingily dressed as yourself, exclaim, 'What a pretty room!' I wish they could see the rooms in my forest. For there are rooms there. Trees whose branches touch the ground, and, taking root again as if they were trees themselves, form bowers so cool and delicious that no one who has lived in one of them could ever be content with such hard dull sides as what you call your walls. The colours of my race, black and white, were much admired by the gorgeous birds, green, gold, and scarlet, who used to keep the forest alive with their chatter—the handsome birds rarely or never sing. Little grey fellows, prettily-enough marked, and with nice red necklaces, were our favourite songsters. You have one in your aviary, and you call him a cutthroat, and think he sings. Ah, you should have heard him in his own land! Our cock birds sing a little, though you might not believe it when you listen to him." She nodded her head towards her despised mate. "He was my companion in my nest, and he was always a poor creature."

He was eating now, glad of her preoccupation. She interrupted herself to take a feather out of his tail, which seemed to cause him considerable annoyance, though he did not attempt to resent it. He only left off eating and crouched down at the bottom of the cage. The talking bird went on :—

"The monkeys were my great friends. They were such amusing fellows. I never went very near them, they used to pull the feathers out of the tails of all the grand birds who were unwary enough to approach them ; and though they professed great friendship for me, I never perched when I talked to them. I used to poise on my wings at a respectable distance, and no entreaties ever got me within reach of their long arms. I used to laugh heartily at the tricks they played on my neighbours, and I even suggested one or two fresh ones. There were some merry little monkeys who were my particular friends, but the funniest sight I ever saw had a very sad ending for some great big monkeys who always imitated every thing that they saw done. I have seen them trying to pick up seeds from the ground like little birds, and perch and hop as birds do; in short, there was no end to the ridiculous antics they played. One day some creatures we had never seen before then—I know now they are men—came into our part of the forest and occupied themselves in very odd ways. They used to rub the branches of the trees with something out of a pot. I took care not to go near these branches, but some of the bright-coloured birds actually perched upon them. They are all stupid, the handsome-plumaged birds. The finer their feathers, the more empty their heads. Some of the little monkeys were foolish enough to go and see what had happened. The branches had been made sticky. Monkeys and gay birds stuck fast. The birds looked like those quiet ones in cases, fixed to their branches. They were too stupid to struggle after their first attempt. The monkeys did all they knew to get away, but their struggles did not avail them; so, after all, the stupid birds who kept still were the best off, for the monkeys added to their misery by making themselves hot with their attempts to get free.

"The horrid men came back again and put the monkeys in bags. The birds were put into cages. How they did beat their poor heads against the bars. I pitied them with all my heart, little thinking I should one day share their fate, but not through my own stupidity." The little bird plumed herself, gave her mate a peck, for the foolish fellow had crept near her to listen to her conversation, and then went on.

"The big monkeys came down and began doing what the men were doing, as nearly as they could. They lifted up the little monkeys and tried to put them in the spare sacks that were lying on the ground; but it required more dexterity than they possessed, and so their intended victims got away. The men took no apparent notice of these big blundering monkeys, and they went away in time with their spoils. Next day they came back again with things in their hands which I know now you call basins, and they did some very odd things with their hands in these basins. You call it washing your hands.

"No sooner had the men gone away than the big monkeys came down to do what they had done, for the men had left their basins behind them. There were six basins, and the monkeys were in such a hurry to be the first to copy the men that two at a time rushed to one basin. Twelve monkeys plunged their long hairy hands into the very bottom of the basins, but they never drew them out again. The men had filled the basins with something even more sticky than what they had spread on the branches, and the poor monkeys were held down, unable to carry out their intention of doing as the men had done, until their cruel deceivers came back, put them into some enormous sacks, and went off making a hideous noise, like the jackals and the hyenas used to make during the night. I thought them all very foolish, and gloried more than ever in my own liberty. Besides my friends the monkeys, I had friends amongst all the birds, and especially amongst the males of my own sort. The females did not care for me; but then I didn't take much notice of them, poor things, and no one else did either when I was present."

Mrs. Mannikin looked so extremely pitiful of others and pleased with herself at this point that Geoffrey had to turn his head away in order to indulge in a quiet laugh.

She thought doubtless that she had made a proper impression, and paused to give it full and due effect. Then she went on :—

" I soon made up my mind which of my little black and white admirers I preferred, but I thought a little suspense would be good for him, so I treated them all with friendly impartiality. The rainy season had now set in. The sun did not show himself for days and days. The gay butterflies, which had rivalled the smart birds for colour, disappeared altogether. The sober night-moths no longer haunted the dusky glades. The great beasts only appeared when hunger drove them out of their dens in search of food. We birds selected the thickest shade, but even by that means did not altogether escape the deluge. The monkeys did not like the wet, but huddled together in any holes they could find, and grumbled and scolded most disagreeably.

" I thought this would be a good moment to smile on the suitor I favoured, but unfortunately the rain had begun so suddenly that we were obliged to take refuge without delay and without choosing our company, and I found myself condemned to the society of my very un-interesting brother. My mother was on our perch, and some funny little yellow finches and a pair of cut-throats, as you call them, filled up the spare room."

CHAPTER XV.

CAPTIVITY.

ELEANOR came in when the twilight was getting very dusky. She looked into the library: Arthur and Mr. Chamberlayne were talking, with open books near them on which the firelight cast a fitful glow. But they had evidently ceased to refer to books, and were drawing on memory's stores.

Arthur looked eager, animated, almost happy; Mr. Chamberlayne was always cheerful, and now he was interested. Miss Norman glided away unnoticed, "in spite of my hobnails," she thought, with a quiet laugh. "I hope my little Geoffrey has not been lonely." She had been detained longer than she had expected. But the bright smiles which greeted her in the sitting-room quite reassured her. "Amie," he exclaimed; "the mannikin is telling me its story, and you must come and write it down. I think I can remember everything, and you must make the words go along nicely, as if it were a book."

Eleanor quite entered into the idea, and sitting between the bird in its cage and the boy on his sofa, she was able to write down exactly what Geoffrey wanted. He made her read the first part over, and listened quite as contentedly as if it had been a new story. Children generally prefer a story that is familiar, and are very particular about having it told in the same words every time.

When his aunt had entirely fulfilled his wishes, he sighed contentedly, and said, " It was rather clever of me understanding the bird. Don't you think so, Amie ? "

" And it is very clever of me writing it down so nicely ; don't you think so, Geoffrey ? "

" You want me to see that it was conceited of me thinking myself at all clever, and so you imitate me, Amie." And the boy made believe to be offended, but uncle Arthur came in, so Geoffrey had to make himself pleasant. There was still a little stiffness about Mr. Norman, or perhaps it would be more fair to say that he was not yet quite at his ease. But as Geoffrey observed this very evening with childish naïveté after his uncle had left the room to dress for dinner, " Uncle Arthur improves every day ; " and Eleanor laughed her assent to the statement as she followed her brother's example, and Natalie came to put Geoffrey to bed.

Next day the bird resumed its position, clinging with its feet to the wires of the cage, and putting its funny little blue bill between them, and Geoffrey prepared to hear what it had to say.

" I saw my friend on another bough, at a considerable distance, sitting curiously enough between his mother and sister, but I must say he looked more contented than I felt. I never try to appear otherwise than I feel, and I was very cross to my brother, and even to my mother,

who I will confess had always been a kind and indulgent
parent to me. Now she did everything she could to
make my position bearable, and in spite of the rain the
cock cut-throat used to sing to his mate at intervals. But
the forest was very dull, and time hung heavily on my
wings. One evening when the rain had abated, though
it was still too heavy to permit us to do more than seek
our daily meals as close to our refuge as possible, those
monsters called men, who had once before disturbed the
happiness of many families in the forest, appeared again.
They came along very quietly; we watched their motions
without moving. We supposed they were going to lime
the boughs again, and we laughed quietly, without, however, giving utterance to the faintest twitter, so I suppose
you would say we smiled. Even the bright-plumaged
stupid birds were not likely to perch again on any
branches these cruel monsters tampered with. The big
and little monkeys ceased grumbling and chattering, and
watched their enemies from their retreats. They would
not be caught with basins and handwashing again, and
the sacks might hunger in vain. They would leave the
forest as thin as they entered it on their grasping owners'
backs for any monkeys they were likely to catch. But
we noticed that our enemies were not provided with
sacks, and it was so dusky in the forest that we could not
see what weapons they held in their hands.

"Only suddenly we found, as we supposed, that the
short but intensely dark tropical night had fallen suddenly,
and it was darkness that we felt too. We were drawn
closer together than we had ever been in our nests, and

we felt as if we could hardly breathe. Was it a thunder-storm? We hoped it might be come to clear the air and restore our usual serene and cloudless sky. Oh, how joyously we anticipated a change in the weather! How we looked forward to sporting with the butterflies and with each other in the sun's returning rays. I determined to take the very first opportunity of dropping a feather, which I meant to extract from my brother's tail, before my favoured suitor. He would of course think it was one of my own, and would prize it accordingly. He would know too that I accepted his attentions, and we should pair, and make our little nest, and in short spend our future life together. I meant him to work for me, and I meant to lead the joyous free life that suited my peculiar nature.

"While these pleasant thoughts were enabling me to bear the disagreeable sensations before described, I felt something take hold of me. I thought a monkey had profited by the darkness, and was going to play on me some of the tricks I had suggested at the expense of others. Suddenly the pressure ceased, and the light appeared with equal suddenness, so that I was quite dazzled. I was almost sure a sunbeam was kissing me. I tried to spread my wings to be the first to enjoy the return of fine weather. Alas, they were as closely folded to my side as when they had been featherless and useless in the once-despised nest. My brother was on one side of me, my mother on the other. The cut-throats and the yellow finches were with us, and we were inclosed in a very small box with wires in front. Through these wires we could see the blessed glorious sun shining down upon us with his broad kindly smile, but we could not even beat our poor wings against our prison, we were so closely packed. I was fortunately placed, if anything could be fortunate under such circumstances. I was nearest the food, such as it was, that was provided for us, and I was protected by my relations from the bills of the cut-throats and the yellow finches. We were all very good friends in the open air, but here in this confined space the different species felt antagonistic, and the strongest let the weakest feel their bills. The cock cut-throat, a very gallant bird, respected my mother's sex, but the hen, perhaps partly on that account, used her very ill. But she had such a charming nature that she contrived to get on the right side of this shrewish bird, and indeed we did not want ill-feeling amongst ourselves to intensify our misery. My poor brother was much pecked by the cock yellow finch, and we should have been thankful now to see less of the sun. His rays increased our sufferings in our confined position. One day a similar prison to ours was placed near us, and I saw my favoured lover in much the same misery as I was in. He contrived however to throw me a note of tender greeting, and I actually divested myself of one of my own feathers, and held it towards him. He was in raptures, and for a few minutes we both forgot our captivity. Our cages were near enough for us to exchange tokens, for of course my friend would not be behind me in proof of devotion, and pulled out his best tail feather.

"We seemed to be making progress in a slow lumbering

was, very unlike our natural fashion, when on free wing we used to cleave the air and sport in the sun's beams. But we had certainly left our beloved forest, after passing through portions that we had not visited when we were free agents. Our course now seemed to lie along a barren sandy plain; the sand got into our prison and added to our discomfort. We had plenty of food, such as it was, and it was certainly fresher than what we get now, and our supply of water was not to be complained of. It was not very sparkling or fresh, but still it was water. Whether we were any the better for this sort of life was a question, but at all events it was well to be spared the tortures of slow starvation from insufficiency of food or water. At last we came to a most curious-looking place. I know now that it was a town, where numbers of human beings gather together, just as tribes of birds congregate. But oh how different to our leafy bowers and our vast general roof of pure blue sky! These human beings inclosed themselves by small companies, varying from two or three to a dozen and more, in hard stone buildings, with dark coverings over their heads. True, some of the walls were relieved by climbing plants, and gay flowers bloomed in most of the windows; but still it was all very uninviting, and we longed more intensely than ever for our own forest, and our precious liberty.

"We never knew before what happiness had meant. We had been content, it is true, but we ought to have been more thankful. I for my part began to repent of the mischievous tricks I had encouraged the monkeys to play, causing annoyance that was unnecessary. Well, I was punished enough now. Our cage was taken into a small dingy building overflowing with human beings, chiefly small by comparison with our captors. They were still monsters in our eyes. These creatures crowded round us curiously and began chattering, reminding me of the parrots and macaws, whose noise in our forest had been a discordant element. Some of these birds, confined like ourselves, added their unmusical tones to the general noise and confusion around us. It was altogether a most uncongenial position. The children, for so we learned these lesser human beings were styled, teased us in every sort of way, until they in turn got what looked very like a teasing from one of the big monsters who had captured us, and we were left alone in our quite-sufficient misery. All these people were black, and, I must admit, some of them were as glossy as our plumage. One day some other men came in with something over their bodies, unlike our captors, who went about without feathers on their persons, though some wore them on their heads. But these new-comers did not wear feathers anywhere. We found out they were sailors. Their faces were not black, but dark brown and red; they looked rather kindly at us, made signs to our captors, gave them some bright berries, or what looked like berries—red, yellow, blue, and green, a sharp thing that glistened in the sun— and, in exchange, one of the party carried off our dingy little cage with its sad freight. Another secured the cage containing my lover, and we had the good-fortune to go in the same direction. We were wonderfully well, it was strange that captivity did not affect our health. Our natural spirits were so high that we actually began to chatter a little, and the cut-throat used to ripple in his throat. He has never done more since he was taken prisoner, you can have no idea of the wonderful beauty and variety of his full song."

The little bird began to scramble round the cage at this point, using bill as well as claws, and Eleanor's pen ceased to "gallop," as Geoffrey described the progress of her writing. "It is very nice," he said, after listening critically to the result of the "gallop," which his aunt read aloud, looking now at the bird and now at Geoffrey, as if she needed approval equally from both.

"It was a very good idea," added the boy, complacently, "and it amuses me very nicely. Do you like it, Amie?"

"Very much, thank you," was the smiling answer; "I quite look forward to the next account. I suppose the bird will describe its journey in the ship."

Geoffrey clapped his hands. "How well you understand." "Yes, I feel sure Mrs. Mannikin will tell us about the ship. I wonder how she liked it. I suppose the town was on the seashore. What do you call it?"

"A seaport," said Eleanor. "Perhaps it was Cape Town."

"I dare say." Geoffrey looked very wise, but he did not know much about Cape Town, except that it was a town in Africa. After all, that is as much, if not more, than many grown-up children know.

10

The little Chamberlaynes came in to have tea with him, but he and Amie agreed that they would keep the bird's story a secret until it was finished, and that then they would read it to everybody as a great surprise.

"Won't they wonder who wrote it down, and how we understood, Amie?" For Geoffrey quite believed in his own story.

CHAPTER XVI.

IN A SHIP.

NOVEMBER was a very changeable month. One day would cheer every one by recalling summer brightness; another would be wild and windy, and a third would begin and end in a steady downpour of rain. Though he could not go out, Geoffrey liked the sunny days; he used to lie in the window with his mannikins beside him, and watch the leaves, bright even in death when the sunbeams burnished up their fading tints. There had been no frosts, consequently the autumn tints were not very brilliant; on the other hand some of the gay autumn flowers, dahlias, China asters, and others, still lent colour to the garden beds.

Eleanor went out in rain and wind as well as in sunshine, and she used to come in with her bright cheeks brightened, and her glad eyes dancing all the more merrily after a successful encounter with " the wild west wind," the " breath of autumn's being," or a good drenching from the pitiless rain.

Sometimes she would run into the rectory, when it was pretty wild, and " not fit for the children to go out," their prudent mother would say; then Eleanor would make a mummy of Fée or Hugh by means of a water-proof cloak which left nothing visible of the little being she came to kidnap, as Mr. Chamberlayne said; then she would put the human bundle on her back like an auld gipsy wife, and run back to the Hall before any one could offer even a laughing remonstrance, and by this means give her own little prisoner in her sitting-room a delightful surprise.

Geoffrey was never well on foggy or wet days. In spite of equal temperature indoors, bright fires and plenty of clothing, the November damp seemed to find its way into his poor little limbs, and they used to ache very severely.

He was patient enough himself, but his uncle used to dread these days of pain for him, and when Geoffrey was suffering Arthur used to have an attack of his old moroseness. "Very hard upon Eleanor," said Lilian, and she set herself to exorcise Mr. Norman's demon. As for Eleanor, nothing ever seemed to depress her, or to weary her, and Geoffrey would say it was quite worth bearing the pain, she relieved it so pleasantly by her delicious rubbing. The professional rubber had taught them how to rub thoroughly, and then they had dispensed with her services. Geoffrey had been very good about it, and he had always been civil and patient, but he had disliked her services very much. His devoted Amie found this out, though he never mentioned it in words, and she set herself with her usual thorough energy to learn the art.

"It is almost as bad as London," says the little

prisoner, watching from the ingle nook the dense fog, which has the one merit of being white instead of yellow.

The little mannikin now diverted his attention and helped him to forget his aching limbs.

"We liked our new captors' faces, but our condition was not improved by the change. We were still huddled together in the little box, and as time went on our food got drier and drier. We saw a very wonderful sight after we had left the town. Before us on the ground, instead of grass, instead even of sand or streets, stretched another sky ! A sky as blue as the one over our heads, curled over with little white clouds, which seemed even more restless than the clouds over our heads. On this blue sky were large dark objects such as we had never seen in our own beloved sky that stretched over our heads in our forest home, and to our great surprise our owners—for they were not our captors, they had got us from them, not from our liberty, so we felt less bitter against them—made for one of these dark objects. I had wanted to reach the sun in my thought-less early youth ; was this the way to the sun ? I had never been able to reach the blue sky on my own wings, how strange to be floating upon it caged up in a wretched box !

" Our owners had got into a sort of open box which they called a boat, and we found the large mysterious objects were called ships. It was very amusing to see the men get from the boat to the ship. How pleased my friends the monkeys would have been to watch and to imitate ! They could not have done it better or

quicker. I began to think there might be some connection between men and monkeys, and I thought I
could like the great monsters better if they recalled my
old familiar friends and playmates. The men found
other men in the ship, and there was a grand display of
treasures rifled from the glorious African forests. The
captain was taking one of our biggest monkeys home
to put it into some gardens in his native land. Some
of the sailors had secured various sorts of little monkeys,
and there were many little boxes like ours full of the
different birds which, free, were one of the glories of our
glorious land. It was not long before the ship began to
move, and the sensation was very curious. Our boxes
were on deck, for the sun was still shining brightly and
warmly."

Mrs. Mannikin looked viciously towards the window
at the dense curling mist, through which the sun had
not even played at penetrating, though he does it in
earnest sometimes, even in November. But Mrs.
Mannikin did not believe in an English sun. However,
she was fond of hearing herself speak, and she soon
continued her story.

"Great white birds used to come and talk to us, and
they told us our ship was sailing. The birds could sail
themselves, and they looked much prettier than the ships
as they sat on the top of this sky, and it looked very
pleasant to glide along with quite a different motion to
flying. Although we were, as I supposed, in the sky, we
never seemed to get any nearer to the sun. Every night
he seemed to roll off the edge of the sky as he used to

do off his bank of clouds when we watched him from our
leafy bowers. Every night the stars came out and shone
brightly for a short time, until the sun appeared from quite
another place than the one from which he disappeared,
and the stars ceased to be visible. At last I found out
that we were on the sea, not the sky, and I found too
that it was not always blue and smooth. Curiously
enough, it used always to be the same colour as the sky.
When the sky was black the sea was black, and so on;
therefore I came to the conclusion that as they were not
the same thing they must be mates. Most certainly they
had paired, as I would so gladly have done with my
dear little lover, whose box was separated from mine by
a great many other boxes. Some of the monkeys used
to be allowed as much freedom as the men, and the
beautiful blue-faced monkey I have spoken of before
looked in at our box one day. There were many of his
sort in the forest, and several amongst the prisoners in
the ship, but I should have known him amongst a thousand. Many a trick he had played under my directions,
and I was quite cheered to see his familiar face grinning
at me. He was so light-hearted that he was quite ready
for mischief anywhere, but he used to think regretfully of
the forest often enough. He used to sigh for freedom,
especially when he got into disgrace with the sailors for
his pranks. When he was caught working the captain's
chart with great gravity, he was shut up for a whole week.
It was said that the ship might have been lost if Mr.
Blueface had not been so much absorbed in his work
that he never heard the captain come into the room, who

thus caught him in the very act. He never meant to be caught, for he knew he was doing wrong. If the ship had been lost we should all have gone below the blue shining sea, which still seemed so like the sky I could not believe that it was black and dreadful inside. Blueface paid his first visit after his release to our box, and I made him very welcome. He never tried to play any tricks upon me, though I was quite at his mercy; but he occasionally extracted a feather from the tails of the other birds, or even from their wings, when they were near enough to the bars. They could not escape, poor things, but they fidgeted so much that they made me quite uncomfortable, and I did not encourage Blueface to tease, as of old. He used to be grave sometimes, particularly when the sea was rough. At first he used to imitate the passengers who suffered from what they called sea-sickness. A very horrid thing it seemed. Blueface used to get a basin and place it on his knees, roll his eyes, hang over this basin and make noises too horrible to bear, while he held his hand to his hairy chest. The sailors, who were not suffering, seemed to be much amused at Blueface's proceedings, and when he ceased to mimic, and succumbed in real earnest to this mysterious and terrible visitation, their merriment increased. I felt quite sorry for my poor funny friend. We birds had troubles enough to bear, but we were spared these sensations, which had such unpleasant results for men and monkeys.

"There was one human being to whom I was specially attracted. Every one behaved as well as they knew how, it never struck any one that the best thing would have been to have released us before we left our own coast. Now it would have been too late. We had left what the sailors called the tropics, where they all felt the heat so severely, which we enjoyed.

" It would have been our turn to have felt the cold, only that we were placed near a horrid black thing that made terrible noises, and spluttered out black and white clouds. It had however the merit of being warm, and when we once experienced what cold meant, after being left too long on deck after the sun went behind a cloud, we got to be quite grateful to this great chimney. It was a sorry substitute for the sun, but it possessed one of its properties, heat. I must tell you about our new friend another day. I am sleepy."

" Mrs. Mannikin called the hen cut-throat a shrewish bird, Amie. I suppose that means hasty in temper."

" Very hasty, I should say," answered Amie.

" I should say our little black friend is shrewish too, then," continued Geoffrey. She was certainly hen-pecking her poor little companion at this moment, and he seemed to have no spirit to defend himself.

" She has evidently had her own way too much," said the aunt. " We must be careful not to spoil you in that style."

Uncle Arthur came in and asked for some tea. He had been out in the fog, and it had chilled and dispirited him.

" Do you think you are going to be ill?" asked Geoffrey, more investigatingly than pitifully.

"I am sure I hope not," said Arthur.   "I shouldn't like it at all."

"No, of course you wouldn't like it.   But it might be good for you.   You would find out then how jolly it is to be able to go out when you like, and never to have aches on foggy days, and you would never look grave when you got all right again."

"I always try not to look grave when I come to see you, Geoffrey."

"You may try, but you don't always succeed.   And then you oughtn't only to smile for me, but you ought to look bright at Amie, as she looks at you; and you ought to say, 'How are you?—fine day—good evening,' and those sort of cheery things that Amie and Mr. Chamberlayne say to the farmers and labourers, and people they meet.   I can tell you they like it.   Their faces shine all over when they get it.   Now you always hurry away when you can, and only just nod when you cannot escape, and I have seen old fellows particularly look so disappointed.   The old woodman said one day when I was able to run about, after you had passed in that grumpy way, 'I can remember Master Arthur as bright and as bonny as the little master here.   And now he goes on greet, greet, and never a smile for any one.'   I asked what 'greet' meant, and Amie told me it was 'being sorry.'   What are you sorry for, uncle Arthur?"   Geoffrey had paused once or twice for want of breath, but getting no answer he had continued to the end.

Amie had left the room to fetch something; she might have been a little dismayed if she had heard her nephew. He had been planning this attack for a long time, and Arthur took it in wonderfully good part.

"I had a great sorrow to bear, Geoffrey," he said, quietly.

"Was it mother's death?"

"That was a sorrow, but it was not the great sorrow."

"But your great sorrow could not be worse than father's when he lost mother, and he didn't change."

Amie came back again and saved Arthur from making an answer, and Geoffrey, young as he was, had tact enough not to carry on such a conversation before a third person, even though that person was his dear and faithful Amie.

CHAPTER XVII.

LAND HO!

THE first touch of frost lay gleaming like manna on lawns and meadows, the gay autumn flowers drooped their heads at last, the remaining leaves were flushed and rosy after this frosty kiss, and the sun was shining brightly. The fires crackled merrily, determined to hold their own, even if the sun should tempt foolish people to open the windows. The fires burnt every day, the sun was very uncertain about his appearance. The fires had been welcome enough only the day before, and now every one rushed to the windows and greeted the sun with delight, while they accepted the fires, even when they wanted them most, as mere matters of course.

Eleanor came into the breakfast-room, where Arthur and Geoffrey were seated, and gave them each a bunch of violets, just as if it were spring. She was a wonderful woman for flowers, and the gardener certainly had every appliance for forcing them. She never was without violets, those sweet heralds of spring, except in mid-summer, when the wealth of summer flowers satisfied her, and the sun was too much for the shy violet. There was no corner shady enough for it, so Eleanor graciously suffered the plants to rest for a couple of months or so. Hitherto she had never got roses before Christmas in her hothouse, it was wonderful how they lingered on and actually flourished out-of-doors in sheltered places until quite the end of November. She had never been without her Christmas roses on Christmas Day. Not only the white low-growing flowers, not unlike wild dog-roses perhaps, but also beautiful June roses, cream-coloured, crimson, and pink.

"I have such a surprise for you, Arthur," she said, as she kissed him and arranged the violets in his button-hole. Arthur was never good at guessing. Geoffrey suggested a litter of pigs, a new calf, a bird's nest. "A bird's nest in November, you little cockney! Well, it is nearly as wonderful." And she slipped out of the door, which she had left ajar, and came in with a fine vigorous young rose-tree in full flower. "And now we shall have them incessantly," she said, triumphantly, "all through the winter and spring. And the stephanotis will be out by Christmas, and the Cape jessamine is nearly in flower."

Both Arthur and Geoffrey shared her enthusiasm, and the latter begged that the rose-tree might be placed quite close to the mannikin's cage. The little persecuted cock ventured to inspect the beautiful thing while Mrs. M., as Geoffrey always called the hen now, was eating her breakfast. Some instinct seemed to tell her that her victim was enjoying himself, she was after him with lightning speed and was occupying his position, which was a convenient one for enjoying both the sight and scent of the gracious flower, which even Mrs. Mannikin considered not unworthy of a place in her own native forest.

Red o'er the forest peers the setting sun,

very early in November, and before the line of yellow light had quite died away, Mrs. Mannikin had taken her favourite position and was glibiy chattering away, catching up the thread of her story just where she had dropped it the evening before.

"The new friend I was going to talk about when I got sleepy was a little girl. She was very little taller than my friend Blueface, the monkey, and she was certainly prettier. Her face was white, just tinted where the monkey's was bluest with a colour like that flower"—Mrs. Mannikin laid her own little black head against the delicate pink petals of the rose which looked in through the bars of the cage. "Her eyes were blue, a deeper blue than the monkey's face, more like the colour of our sky, far deeper than yours"—and the bird just glanced at the frosty sky, which Geoffrey thought quite beautiful— "and her hair, oh, it was like the sun ! It shone so that I felt it must be warm."

Mrs. Mannikin almost involuntarily peeped at Geoffrey's curls, which the rays of the setting sun were burnishing into something very suggestive of gold. Eleanor knew that the bird admired her pet, but he was quite uncon- scious of having made an impression on the sharp- tempered ladykin.

"The ship was full of people besides the sailors, who used to run about and climb the masts, and these people

seemed to have nothing to do. When it was rough, they
rolled about and made horrid noises, but they generally
disappeared on these occasions; while on fine days
they walked slowly, or lay full length on cushions, sometimes in the sailors' way, and then they had to move.
My little friend seemed a general favourite with every one.
She used to run as fast as the sailors, and she seemed to
enjoy a rough day quite as much as a smooth one; but
her greatest delight was watching us in our cages. She
seemed very sad at first to think we should have so little
room to move, but the sailors assured her we did not
mind it. I should like them to have tried it for themselves before they spoke for us. However, we could
not help looking happy when she was watching us, so
that it was not unnatural that she should believe them.
We chirped and talked to her, and she quite seemed to
understand what we said to her ; and the cut-throat rippled
a little song whenever she came near. She thought it
beautiful, and one of the sailors told her she would hear
a song something like it in England, from a bird he
called a nightingale. There is not a bird in England
who could sing as our cut-throat sings in his own forest.
I must admit I have heard better singers than he is now,
even in your land ; but the dear little lady seemed quite
satisfied with the faint strains. One day, when we were
drawing near the end of our sea-voyage, I heard the
sailor who was her particular friend offer her a pair of
birds. She danced about with delight. I thought it
looked prettier than flying or swimming; she hardly
seemed to rest upon her feet, as she darted hither and

thither, before sitting down in front of our long row of prisons, to choose her pair of birds.

"'I should like you all, you darlings,' she said, and we each in turn hoped to be selected; but at last she fixed on a cage at the very end of the line, which evidently contained a single pair, because the sailor said, 'I think you have chosen well, little missy, and there will be no separating.' Then she had not chosen my chosen mate for one of her pair, for his cage was as full of different sorts as mine was. Oh! if she had only chosen him out of his cage and me out of mine! I always used to think she took particular notice of me, except, of course, when the cut-throat was singing. As she passed me with the tiny cage in her hand, I saw that she had selected a pair of cut-throats. Oh, for a voice, even changed and feeble as theirs was to our ears! I would have sung unceasingly, and found strength to reproduce the old clear forest-strains, if I might have belonged to her. Our ship was now in what the sailors called harbour; stone walls inclosed the sea, and other ships greeted our ship. There were a good many ships in this harbour, and strangers came to our ship. We were kept apart, however, for a time, and some one used a very long word about us. I found that it meant not mixing with others until it was ascertained beyond doubt that there was no illness amongst our crew. My pretty little friend was very anxious to get out of the ship. She had come home to her native land, which she had, however, never seen. How could it be home if she had never seen it? I could not understand then. Now I suppose, if we were to

make a nest in our cage, and bring up some young ones
here, if any good luck took them to our native forest it
would be home to them, though they were not born there.

"Every one said the weather was fine. We found it
chilly, especially when were we left too long in what the
sailors called 'sunshine.' We liked our black funnel
better. The sunshine was very pale, and the wind
was very cold. The little lady seemed to flourish,
however. Her pink cheeks got pinker, while my poor
old friend Blueface lost the beautiful deep tint which
had made his face so remarkable, and he looked almost
grey, paler than the new sky, which we thought a very
poor exchange for our deep blue native sky. The
monkeys were all in coats like the men, the sailors
dressed them in their old clothes. I wonder they liked
to do it. It made the monkeys look so like them, and
my pretty little friend was never tired of laughing at
them. One monkey was dressed up in an old petticoat
and jacket that had belonged to her, but it did not make
the monkey look a bit like her, I was glad to see. The
great big monkey had grown very cross during the journey; he never had been particularly good-tempered, and
I think his master was very glad to give him in charge to
a man who came for him to put him in a wonderful
garden, which my little lady seemed very anxious to
visit. I wondered what this garden could be like, and
whether it would remind poor old cross Mr. Monkey of
his own dear forest. I have every reason to believe that
it is a poor-enough place, though every care is taken of
the birds and beasts that live there."

Mrs. Mannikin used always to stop just when Geoffrey wanted her to go on. He was longing to hear what she thought of England when she got out of the ship, but she wanted her tea, and she never spoke after that meal.

"Don't you long for the next chapter, Amie?" he said, with a sigh, as his aunt wiped her pen.

"Very much," she said, quite gravely. "But don't you know that anticipation is a great pleasure in itself?"

"I don't know what anticipation means."

"An-ti-ci-pa-tion. It is a long word. It means to look forward with pleasurable expectation."

"Well done, Amie," said Arthur, coming in at that moment. "Are you going to write a dictionary? Let us see how Dr. Johnson, the grim authority, describes the word. 'To anticipate, to prevent, to foretaste. Anticipation, the act of taking up something before its time; prevention.'"

"A very bad explanation," said Eleanor, decidedly. "My authority is Chambers."

"Let us refer to Mr. Chambers then." Arthur read out, "To anticipate (from the Latin *anti*, before, *capio*, to take), to foretaste, to foresee. Anticipation, foretaste, previous notion." "Well, I think that is a better definition. But pleasurable is a word that should be added. It is not included in the hidden meaning. There are such things as unpleasing anticipations."

"Well, Arthur, you have got the best of me, and the feminine privilege of the last word into the bargain," said Eleanor, good-temperedly.

"But Amie always does expect, anticipate pleasant things, so she only explained the word as she acts it," said Geoffrey.

"Well done, little champion," was his uncle's pleased comment.

"Uncle Arthur improves so much, he will soon be as nice as he need be," was Geoffrey's confidence to his aunt while she was dressing for dinner.

Hitherto, though they had never been made welcome, a few neighbours, who could not exist without exchanging visits, especially with the great people of the neighbourhood, had called occasionally. Eleanor, genial and hospitably inclined, had received them kindly and had returned their visits, furtively dropping Arthur's card on their Hall tables. She never confessed what she did, and as the empty compliment pleased the worthy householders, and did not draw Arthur into closer connection with them, in his most churlish days he could hardly have resented such a very cheap expression of civility. Nevertheless, Eleanor carefully pounced upon all the return cards, and wound her silks upon them, for fear Arthur should suspect her and forbid her to continue leaving his card unknown to him.

Now all this was wearing off, and he had been in his own person to pay one or two visits. The Chamberlaynes often dined at the Hall, and Mr. Chamberlayne having expressed a wish to meet a scientific neighbour who had not happened to call at the rectory during his tenancy, Arthur actually volunteered to ask him to dinner.

Eleanor, with her usual tact, treated the proposal as if it were an everyday occurrence; and as the scientific man had a pleasant wife and daughter, they must be invited as a matter of course. Then a nearer neighbour had an observatory of which Mr. Chamberlayne desired to have the run, and it ended in Arthur bringing upon himself, by his own act, a party of country neighbours.

CHAPTER XVIII.

IMPRESSIONS OF ENGLAND.

PEOPLE are often more ashamed of themselves for doing what is right if it brings about a change in their ways and attracts notice than they are of going on in their old bad ways. This was certainly the case with Arthur Norman. After he had made up his mind to the dinner-party he looked as if he had committed, or at least intended to commit, some great crime. But Eleanor took it all as a matter of course, an everyday occurrence, and the servants took their cue from her.

"We shall be fourteen to dinner," she said to the butler.

"Very good, ma'am," he answered, as if such a thing did not surprise him in the least.

The old housekeeper did say, "That's right, my dearie, it is time some one was seeing your bonny face."

Geoffrey is in a great state of excitement. His parents used to have dinner-parties he believed, but he had generally, if not always, been in bed when they came off.

Eleanor is writing the invitations the day the matter has been settled. Lilian is sitting near her watching her busy pen and laughing at the matter-of-fact way in which she invited people who had not enjoyed Normanhurst hospitality for seven years. " I know Lady Felton is at the sea, though she is expected back directly, so I will write to Sir William."

" I did not know it was a case of the bloody hand ; I thought it was a K.C.B., or whatever letters distinguish a knight of learning," said Lilian.

" Oh, my dear, what ignorance ! He is a Nova Scotia baronet, and would, I verily believe, decline a modern peerage."

" I honour him for that. I am tired of these perpetual new peers; it is almost impossible to make out who people are."

Geoffrey was learning his French lesson in his quiet corner, and was really trying not to listen to his aunt and her friend ; but the case of the bloody hand attracted or distracted his attention in spite of himself, and he devoutly hoped he should not have to shake hands with the guest so afflicted. " I suppose he covers it up," he thought, as he resolutely returned to his task.

Arthur came in and Eleanor said, " Are you going into the town to-day ? "

" I am thinking of it," was the somewhat short answer.

" Then, dear, you had better call at the barracks, the new regiment has not been there long, and I know the names of the most passable or presentable of the officers. We must have some men for our two young ladies."

Arthur looked as if he would sooner have called at the

gaol and bidden a murderer and a pickpocket to his feast, but he only said he had not got any cards.

"Here are plenty," said Eleanor, briskly.

Lilian was obliged to look out of the window so that Arthur might not see her smile. She began to hum, quite unconsciously, "Oh comme j'aime les militaires," when Geoffrey said,—

"Do you? Then why did you marry a clergyman? Does Amie like the soldiers too?"

Arthur was obliged to laugh, and Eleanor said, "I shall tell Mr. Chamberlayne of her, Geoffrey."

"No, don't, Amie, you always tell me not to repeat things, it may do harm, by not being repeated in the same way, and sometimes, even if it is, it makes too much of it to say it again."

"Well done, Geoffrey," said Lilian. And then Arthur and she went their several ways. Amie proceeded to the housekeeper's room and kitchen, according to her wont, and Geoffrey mastered his poem and did his lessons to Natalie's entire satisfaction.

Mrs. Mannikin was very interesting that evening.

"After the dear little lady went away with the fortunate birds she had chosen, I felt very melancholy. I saw the cage containing my lover carried off, and then Blueface left the ship with his owner. At last our turn came, and our owner, a young fellow with a kind face, put our cage bodily into his pocket. We did not see much of the land in consequence at first, but we made such an angry twittering in our dark prison that a crowd soon gathered round our thoughtless owner, and made such a noise as

I thought would have drowned our feeble remonstrance. Something however had the effect of releasing us, and we were carried the rest of the way through the open air. Every one said the weather was charming. We thought it cold, but the air was very sweet, and the trees were covered with something white, delicately tinted with pink. Our owner said, 'What a grand promise of apples.' 'Ay, ay,' said another he called his mate.

"The birds sang very delightfully, I must admit, and there was one bird in particular whose song was so joyous that we all felt as if we must soar when we heard it, even if we dashed out our brains in the effort against the roof of our prison. This bird soared while he sang.

"'None of them foreign birds can match the skylark,' said our owner.

"'The cut-throat could have beaten him,' I thought; but certainly the skylark had a very delightful song of his own. We spent the first night of our arrival in England at a little house all covered with sweet climbing plants, which, though they did not equal the glories of our climbers, had a fair delicate beauty of their own which we did not despise.

"A woman received our owner very warmly. She folded him up, cage and all, in her arms, and pressed her bill to his, as I longed to press mine to that of the dear little mate who was—ah, where? Perhaps not faring so well as we were. There were some little girls here, and, though they were very different to my little lady on board the ship, they were pleasant and kindly enough.

"The master of the house, who came in shortly after, was

a bird-fancier, and he was much delighted with the small collection his son had brought home from Afric's sunny clime. Some one called it a sultry clime, but it was never too hot for us. Some more cages were soon found. My mother, my brother, and I were put into one, the yellow finches into another, and the cut-throats into a third. 'They know something,' I thought, as I noticed how wisely we were divided; and I chose the best perch for myself and stretched out my wings. We all felt very odd when we had more room, almost uncomfortable, we had got so used to our close quarters, and certainly cold. The bird-fancier named us; we were mannikins, our friends with the coral necklaces were cut-throats, and the funnily marked yellow fellows he called singing finches. They twittered a little certainly, but not better than we did. We got as near together as we could after the first, and watched all the strange proceedings that went on around us. Suddenly the mother of our friend said, ' Hush, the nightingale concert is beginning.'

"And we heard the world-famous singers. The cut-throat said he never could equal those varied strains, even in his happiest days, and he had never heard such a song from the best singer of his tribe. It rippled and purled like a stream, then rose higher and higher, until it became triumphant, to die away in a faint though still perfectly musical jug, jug, jug. The young sailor had something in his eyes which made them shine, as he said, ' Oh, mother, it is worth all the pain of going away to be amongst you all again and to hear that concert.' We almost thought that in spite of captivity, cold, dry food,

we could understand what the sailor meant, and we
certainly enjoyed the nightingale concert as much as he
did."

"The little shrew has some nice ideas, Amie, hasn't
she?" said Geoffrey, as Mrs. Mannikin fluttered away to
take her evening meal, and Amie put away her writing
materials. It is the day of the dinner-party. Geoffrey is
to wear his velvet suit and see the people arrive. He is
to sit in his little chair, not lie down, which is a great
advance for him.

The company are received in the music-hall, and they
are to dine in the large dining-room. Every one has
accepted, and Geoffrey hopes and trusts that the gentleman with the bloody hand will have it carefully covered
up. Amie is in the room, dressed in white, with pearls
round her neck, and a real camellia in her hair. Geoffrey
thinks she looks very beautiful, as he watches her putting
finishing touches to the arrangement of her flowers and
pretty things. Mrs. Chamberlayne comes in now,
followed by her husband and by Arthur. She is in
black velvet, which suits her fair skin, though it does
not give her the matronly air she aspires to. There is
a wonderfully youthful appearance about this mother of
four children. Arthur has determined to endure his
penance like a man and a Briton, and he does not look
more gloomy than the ordinary English host on such an
occasion.

Lilian admires Geoffrey's velvet suit, and then the door
opens and two young officers are announced. For the
life of him Geoffrey cannot help softly humming the

famous air out of the Grande Duchesse, which must have been very familiar to the two military thus greeted. One of them, a young sub, with a merry rosy face, made friends with Geoffrey on the spot, after getting through the more formal introductions to the elders.

Then came the owner of the observatory and his family. He was immediately introduced to Mr. Chamberlayne, and they began talking as if they had known each other all their lives. No hero with a wounded hand so far. " Perhaps it is too bad for him to come," thought Geoffrey, half relieved, half disappointed. He had a great dislike to the sight of wounds, at the same time he was very curious to see " a case of the bloody hand," and a Nova Scotia baronet. Every one has arrived except the Feltons.

Amie begins to wonder if the scientific man has forgotten all about his engagement, Geoffrey hopes he is not at that critical moment bleeding to death, when the door opens again, and Sir William, Lady, and Miss Felton are announced.

Sir William carries his right hand in the breast of his waistcoat. " That is the bloody one," thought Geoffrey. " I hope he shakes hands with his left ; it would not be rude if he has hurt his right hand."

But no ; out comes the right hand, without a bandage or any suggestion of court-plaister, and grasps his aunt's hand warmly.

" It must be the left hand after all," thinks Geoffrey, busily pursuing his meditations.

By this time Sir William has found his way to the ingle

nook. "And this is Marian's boy," he is saying to Eleanor; "I think I should have known him anywhere." And taking Geoffrey's hands in both his he kisses him warmly. After a careful inspection of both the hands thus holding his, Geoffrey exclaimed, apparently irrelevantly, "I am so glad your hand is well. I was afraid when you were late that you might be bleeding to death."

Sir William started at this singular greeting, but Eleanor remembered in a moment what had passed between Lilian and herself on the subject. Geoffrey did not, however, give her time to explain, for he went on, "I don't think you can be the man they were speaking of, for they said you were a Nova Scotia barrow something. Now I know Nova Scotia is an island close to America, and you are an Englishman."

This speech gave Sir William a clue to the boy's mistake, and when Amie could speak for laughing she cleared up the whole mystery.

"Little pitchers have long ears and very fertile imaginations," she added, as she took Sir William's arm to follow the rest of the company in to dinner.

The meal proved a very pleasant one, and the party was altogether a success. Sir William and Lady Felton invited the Chamberlaynes to dine and sleep at their house the following week; it was settled, however, that they could only dine, and Arthur and Eleanor would bring them in their carriage.

Arthur was going to dine out again. He felt it was no use doing things by halves, and he really had enjoyed his evening so much, he felt that he had been foolish as well as selfish in making the worst of his trouble for so long. There was no doubt he had been selfish in depriving Eleanor of society and society of Eleanor, they suited each other so perfectly.

The officers both fell in love with her, but she was ungrateful enough never to know which was which during their whole stay in the neighbourhood.

In vain Geoffrey urged the superiority of his friend over the other; Amie did not deny it, but she could never realise it. Lilian defended the military, as in duty bound after her musical profession on the subject, and altogether the dinner-party marked the commencement of a new era in life at Normanhurst.

CHAPTER XIX.

ANOTHER CHANGE.

AT breakfast next morning Geoffrey was full of questions. In the first place he had not arrived at the explanation of the meaning of Nova Scotia baronet, and of the bloody hand. It was all very well for Amie and the very pleasant gentleman with perfectly sound hands to laugh, he was quite as much puzzled as ever.

"The bloody hand is the badge of the baronets," explained Arthur, for the recollection of the scene made Eleanor laugh too heartily to speak. "You know this seal with bars, and stripes, and men, which in heraldry are called supporters—well, the baronets are entitled to add to all these devices the badge of the bloody hand."

"What a nasty badge. I am glad you have not got one, uncle Arthur. But I don't quite understand what a coat-of-arms is good for. It does not keep you warm?"

"No, it is a distinction, and 'heraldry,' which explains it, is a science which its students find absorbing, and which really requires a good deal of application to master thoroughly."

"It is always suggestive of the middle ages," said Eleanor, "and therefore it has attractions for me."

"Then the Nova Scotia barrow?"

"Baronet," corrected Arthur. "Baronet is a title, a higher distinction than knight. Sir William Felton, Bart. is a greater man than Sir Gregory Stubbs, Knight, late Lord Mayor of our ancient town, though I do not suppose the latter thinks so. Nova Scotia is a distinction too, it signifies the oldest creation of baronets."

"It is rather interesting," said Geoffrey, "but I don't quite understand."

"You must wait till you are older, and then we will study the subject thoroughly," said his uncle.

"By the way," said Geoffrey, relieved to have done with such a profound subject for the present, "I asked Ray to come and see the house, and I promised to take him over it, he says he does not like going with the regular sight-seers on the public days. I am afraid I shall hardly be able to walk all over, so I dare say you will show him over, Amie."

"Who is Ray?" asked Eleanor.

"That nice officer who dined here last night."

"There were *two* nice officers—which is Ray?"

"Oh dear no!" said Geoffrey, superior as having tested the merits of the military. "Smith was a stupid fellow, but Ray was very jolly."

"Well then I hope the jolly one will not bring the stupid one, as I suppose you will talk to the former and leave me to entertain the latter."

But officers have a habit of calling in couples, and the

two who had dined at Normanhurst came as in duty
bound to call there. Geoffrey received Ray warmly, but
he evidently felt Amie was bound to entertain Smith.
" I never asked *him*," he said, convinced that the two
were presuming on his special invitation to Ray.

However, Eleanor was very cordial, and took them
over the house, though Geoffrey shouted after her with
rather an accent on the name, "Mind you tell Ray all
the stories, he is awfully fond of old family stories."

After this call was over Mrs. Mannikin went on with
her story. "I must admit that we were not unhappy
in the cottage. We were treated very kindly, we had got
so used to real confinement that the increase of space
seemed a sort of comparative liberty. True I used to
feel very sad when I saw the cut-throat and his mate
enjoying themselves, and I pined for my little black and
white lover. I was indifferent to my mother, and she
now cared more for my brother than for myself. He was
certainly more attentive to her, and he deserved her
kindness. She pined secretly for her own mate, who
had not been taken prisoner when the rest of us were
captured. He was probably enjoying life thoroughly in
our own dear forest. Most likely he had forgotten all
about us, and had probably paired with a very attractive
little lady mannikin of about my age, to whom he used
to pay fatherly attentions when we were all together. She
had lost her parents before she could fly far enough to
get her own food, and both my parents had been very
kind to her. I vexed my mother by saying I thought it
would be very well if my father had consoled himself for

the loss of his wife by taking this little orphan under his wing. The coolness between us increased, and I should have been very lonely if I had not made friends with one of the children in the cottage. She was not pretty at all, and she walked unevenly and heavily, but she had a kind face, a gentle voice, and nice ways altogether. I am sure we understood each other; she used to sit near my cage, and I told her the story of my life. I had heard her repeating to herself the story of another life and it began,—

> My life you ask of—well, you know
> Full soon my little life is told,
> It has had no great joy or woe.

"It seemed that my little life, though it might be soon told, could be equally divided. I had known great joy, and I had equally experienced bitter woe.

"The little sick girl seemed to find plenty of joy in her life; every one was so kind to her, so tender of her, that she used to say she was better off as a cripple than most people were who were well. She only wished for one thing, which she hoped to get some day, and she was content to wait for that. It was something beyond the sun and moon and stars, it was something that could not be seen, and I could not wish for anything I could not see. The days grew longer and the sun shone more brightly, but it never recalled itself as I had known it of old, in these my new quarters. The sky was blue, but so pale compared to the roof that spanned our forest!

"At last our sailor friend had to go away, and shortly after that I lost my little lame friend. I suppose she

12

went to the place she longed for, and got the thing she so much wished to possess. The other children were quiet for a little while after she went away, and the parents were sad for all the rest of the time we stayed with them.

"One day a man came into the house, and he looked at us and talked about us, but the woman shook her head, and the children said, ' Oh, we could not part with brother's birds; and Tiny'—that was the little cripple who had gone away later than the sailor brother—'loved them so dearly.'

"We hoped that we should not have to go away, we were really contented now, and had almost forgotten what it was to be free. But when the father came in and heard that what the mother called gold had been offered for us he said times were hard and were likely to get harder, that if the man came again his offer must be taken and we must go away. For his part the birds recalled the little lass, and made him miss her more, and he would rather part with the birds than see them die. Folks said they never lived over a winter in England.

"What did 'die' mean, and what did 'winter' mean?

"The man did come again, and gave gold, and took us all away. We were put back in the dreadful little box cages. The gold was very small and lay quite still when the man who took us put it in the woman's hand. She did not seem to care for it, but looked at us with water shining in her eyes. The children made a great fuss, but our new owner got into a thing drawn by some great animals with four legs, quite unlike any of our big beasts who used to run on four legs, and we ceased to hear the children's voices. Besides, the thing we were in made a noise which prevented our hearing anything else.

"Presently we arrived at a curious place something like the piers where we had embarked and landed, but there was no sea, and a great black monster ran alongside the pier. We were put into this monster, which made a noise like our friendly black funnel that had kept us warm on board ship, and soon we were running along faster than when we were drawn by the animals. We went faster than the birds could fly, faster than the ship had sailed, and I began to wonder if this was the way to the sun. It was a black way, and we seemed to be getting farther and farther from its light and heat. At last we reached a great black town; our new owner proceeded on his own legs through some streets, carrying our cage, and we soon found ourselves in a dingy dark room quite full of birds and beasts and all kinds of curious things. The first person I recognised was my old friend Blueface."

As usual Mrs. Mannikin got hungry at an exciting moment, and she climbed down by the wires of her cage to partake of her evening meal before she retired for the night.

"I do hope the Chamberlayne children will like the story," said Geoffrey, with a little sigh of content, while Amie put away her writing things. "I think it might

12 *

interest uncle Arthur; he always liked the birds, even before he got so very nice. He liked them even when he was not at all nice, didn't he?"

Eleanor said that Arthur had always liked birds from his earliest boyhood, and that even when he had been very sad indeed (she laid a stress on the word sad) he had been interested in the well-doing of the birds.

"People are sometimes nice when they are sad?" said Geoffrey, in a slightly interrogative voice.

"They can never be cheerful if they give way to sadness. And I suppose you think people are not nice who do not laugh and talk."

"You don't think dull people nice yourself, Amie," said Geoffrey, in his little decided voice.

"Talk of a woman fighting for the last word—you are champion at that game, my little Geoffrey."

"What does champion mean?" he asked.

"The winner, or the best man. Here come tea and uncle Arthur. Shall I tell him what you said about him?"

"No, no," said Geoffrey; "you do not like me to say everything you say about people, even if it is no harm."

"But I want to know what makes those little cheeks so rosy, not to say fiery," said uncle Arthur.

"Will you tell him yourself, Geoffrey?" said Eleanor, mischievously.

"Well, uncle Arthur," said Geoffrey, who really was a champion in its sense of hero when it came to being straightforward, "I asked Amie about you before you became so nice as you are now, and I asked her whether you cared for birds when you were not nice at all. You know I really did not care for you all the time in London. I began to like you when we bumped noses in the train, and I have gone on liking you better and better, and now I really like you very much indeed."

"Thank you, Geoffrey," said his uncle, in a funny dry voice. These wholesome truths must have been a little trying sometimes, but he really took them in wonderfully good part.

"Don't you think you had better get on with your tea, my very loquacious nephew?" said Eleanor.

"What does lo—lo— mean?" asked the irrepressible nephew, and then, *sotto voce* to his uncle, "She always uses long words when she is vexed.

Arthur, relieved by the tables being turned on his sister, though she had suffered on his behalf, explained graciously.

"Loquacious means very talkative; saying a great deal on a subject."

"I do like talking," said Geoffrey, quite contentedly; "and I can talk while I am eating."

"Loquacious means talking too much, and that is quite as bad as doing anything too much—eating too much, or playing too much, or doing too much French," added Amie, mischievously.

She always corrected her nephew in this practical way. She never scolded, never lectured, and yet she always made him feel when he did wrong. Sometimes he would go on, as he had done on this occasion, to try and cover

the reproof, but at her knee he would confess his little
sin and repent of it.

He rarely erred in the same way again, and she never
had to punish him.   He would have minded a punish-
ment less.   When he grieved his kind Amie he was
always sad until he had set the matter right.

"Do you think uncle Arthur minded what I said?"
he whispered, after he had finished his evening hymn.

"You know he did, dear; but I know you will never
talk in that way again.   I had told you he had gone
through a great sorrow, a sorrow that may come to you
some day, and. if he did not bear it well at first he
deserves all the more credit for bearing it well now."

"And will he be sorry all his life about one thing?"
asked Geoffrey, wonderingly.

"I hope not, I hope he may find out in time that it is
no longer a sorrow.   I think he is finding it out slowly.
And now good night, my little forgiven boy."

Could such a sorrow ever cloud her boy's bright young
life?   To see him was to love him; to know him was to
well-nigh worship him.   Amie prayed, as his lips clung
to hers in a long lingering kiss, that he might be blessed
in his love all his life long,

CHAPTER XX.

THE RESULT OF A SIN OF OMISSION.

GEOFFREY was getting better faster than any one had expected. A very damp day came in the beginning of December, and he felt no pain at all in his legs; his back was a little weak still, but he was able to sit up without fatigue for a longer time each day.

He was looking forward with great pleasure to a concert his aunt was arranging. It was to take place in the music-room, and he would wear his velvet suit, and if he were to lie down a good deal that day he might sit up for the concert, and no one would know he had ever been a little sick boy. Hugh and Fée were to come, of course; and Lilian would sing, and Amie would play for every one, and she would play a splendid piece on the organ by herself. Uncle Arthur begged for that, and every one else pressed her eagerly to fulfil his wish.

Eleanor always believed people meant what they said, and they really did mean it in this case. She consented to play by herself as pleasantly as she had arranged to accompany all the songs and choruses.

Geoffrey was too much excited to think about anything

except the coming event for the days immediately preceding the concert, but the evening before, after a hard morning's practice, Amie and he were sitting doing nothing for half an hour before tea, so Mrs. Mannikin very obligingly went on with her story.

"Our new home had one merit, it was very warm. I should say it was quite as warm as our native land. It was a more even heat than the neighbourhood of the funnel on board ship, and we felt if we could only see the sun and blue sky that we might be in another part of our own forest. In a cage very high up I saw my dear little friend for whom I had pined all this time, and he knew me at once and made signs of recognition. Blueface had a chain round his leg, but it was a long one, and he was able to come close up to our cage and tell us his adventures since we had parted. They interested me at the time, but were neither remarkable nor exciting, and I have quite forgotten what they were. He was not looking very well, poor fellow, but his spirits never quite failed him.

"We were tolerably well attended-to considering how many there were of us. We had been settled for several lights and darknesses in our new home (what you call days and nights), the latter very long and the former grey and dull, when a man came into the shop and asked to look at us. Many people came and went, a very few went away empty-handed, but hitherto no one had noticed us. This man after a very short time bought us all. He gave gold, more gold than had been given to the poor woman, and in exchange he carried off our cage

and its contents.   More travelling in the black monster
that ran along without being drawn by animals ; we had
a peep of sunshine now and again, and at last we found
ourselves in this room.   It was warm and pleasant, and
bright too, compared to our late quarters.   You know
how we were arranged, my mother and the cut-throats
and the yellow finches all in a place like a tiny imitation of our forest.   When we visit them they seem
tolerably contented, and my mother has found a mate, I
see.   My brother grows more dull and stupid every day.
I think he will soon try what dying is like for a change.
I have heard people say a bird has died, and I have seen
it lying so stiff and still I do not feel at all inclined to
try the experiment.   Over our cage I noticed a little
being shaped like a boy, but so small I could not make
out what it was.   It seemed to be flying, but I knew that
could not be the case, for no creature of his size could
have been supported on such short wings.   Our wings
are longer than our whole bodies."   And Mrs. Mannikin
stretched out her pretty black wings and looked very
wise.

" The little figure used to swing round and round, and
at last I saw a thin wire from the middle of its body by
which it hung from the wall. I found out that it was only
an ornament, like all the other things in the room.   At
first I hoped it might be a little companion, and I used
to talk to it, but it never took any notice.   Of course it
couldn't.   I like talking to you, but I have not much
more to tell you ; you know more about what you do
yourself than I can tell you ; and for my part, after the

many changes in my life, I find it dull and quiet here. It is comfortable, and generally warm, and there is plenty to eat of a dry sort; and when I have said that, I have said all there is to say on the subject." Mrs. Mannikin looked critically at Geoffrey and then turned her back on him, knocked her poor mate out of the seed-place, where he was hastily swallowing his evening meal, took her own leisurely, and made herself, as usual, very comfortable.

"I should say she is a very selfish bird," said Geoffrey; "She only seems to care for herself. I wonder, if she had her own mate, whether she would be nicer to him."

Eleanor was very seldom in a hurry, and consequently she never fussed. Everything was in due order, tea was prepared for the performers, to be followed, after the entertainment, by supper, at which the "quality" intended to preside. She had always given a concert every winter, but this was the first held in the house. Arthur had proposed it himself, and had not looked preoccupied, let alone gloomy or morose, since the affair had been settled. He and Mr. Chamberlayne were going to give a funny dialogue, Geoffrey's friend Ray was found to be talented in that way, and one or two other performers in the same line volunteered to vary the vocal and instrumental character of the entertainment.

It only wants half an hour to the preliminary flourish. The choir are having their tea, at which Amie and Geoffrey, and Lilian and her two eldest children are presiding. The gentlemen are dining in the small dining-room. Eleanor is too wise to upset them by putting them off with tea when she wants them all to be at their best. No one has grumbled, and though Lilian's cheeks are pinker than usual, and Eleanor looks a little pale, they both smile and chat merrily, and the children are wild with excitement and anticipation. The choir take their tea silently; eating is a business, and a serious business of life, with them. They answer when they are spoken to, and laugh at the children's sallies, and the meal proceeds pleasantly.

The butler and housekeeper are in the great music-hall putting finishing touches to the arrangements, which seem perfect enough as they are. Great branches of wax candles light every corner thoroughly, and still there is no unpleasant glare, as in a gas-lit room. The great dogs at each end are well plenished with logs of wood, and secretly kept alight with a concealed bed of coal; the flowers are beautiful, and the room smells of summer.

"It is like old times," said the grey-haired butler, who quite recalled the venerable seneschal of the past in his bearing and manners.

The aged housekeeper sighed and said, "It can never be the same again. I would not be for having the dear old people back again "—Mrs. Dene had been a girl when old Mr. and Mrs. Norman had been young people. "They did their work well, they have earned their reward. But to think we shall never see Miss Marian again, never hear her voice filling this great hall again—oh, it makes my old heart ache."

"We must not be for calling her back, any more than the old people," said Dene, solemnly. The butler and housekeeper had married in middle life, and a very comfortable arrangement it had proved for themselves, as well as for their master and mistress.

"I mind the last time she sang in this old hall was after Master Geoffrey's christening. She sang, 'I know that my Redeemer liveth,' and Miss Norman, she played the music for her. It seemed as if she did feel what she sang, and I felt as if it was almost heaven then. She made it blessed for us all when she was on earth, and she has gone from a sweet life here to the perfect peace and joy of heaven."

Mrs. Dene quietly wiped her eyes, and her husband went to the door, after patting her kindly on the shoulder. The first bell had rung, and the guests followed in quick succession. The room was soon full, and Eleanor opened the proceedings with the promised piece on the organ.

Then followed glees, solos, recitations (grave and gay); and every one agreed that the entertainment came to an end much too soon.

The children were just allowed to see the goodly gathering sit down to supper in the great banqueting-hall, and then they went to bed to live the whole glad evening over again in their dreams.

That supper was a most successful entertainment. Arthur talked as brightly as Eleanor did; gentle and simple were at their ease; and people felt, though they did not say it, that Mr. Norman was at last rewarding his sister for her long patience, and finding out how easy it was to be happy. The sight and sound of happiness, merry faces, cheerful voices—innocent enjoyment, in short, is an ample reward for any trouble.

Eleanor had very early in life found the philosopher's stone. It is a jewel that no Indian mine can produce, no chemic art can counterfeit. It is brighter than gold, more precious than the diamond. She possessed a cheerful contented spirit. She made the happiness of others her object in life; she lived for others, and so it was a pleasure to live. She cared for the good of others, and so her own life was full of good. But she had neglected one duty on the day of the concert, and she had to repent it in deep humiliation. It was her pleasant duty to cover up the cage which contained Geoffrey's precious mannikins every night; and she never forgot it, because she was always in her sitting-room when the proper time for shrouding the cage arrived. But on the afternoon of the concert she did not go into her peculiar sanctum, and Geoffrey was not there either; the next morning they were all rather late, and when the delayed breakfast had come to an end, and Lilian and Eleanor went to the sitting-room to talk over the concert, followed by the children, they found the poor little cock mannikin sitting at the bottom of the cage all in a fluff. The hen was quite lively, and was eating her breakfast contentedly. Eleanor remorsefully recollected that she had forgotten to cover the cage as she took her poor little victim out of his pretty prison and tried to warm him in her hands. But it was too late, and the little mannikin died as she held him to her cheek.

His life since he had been in confinement had not been

very bright, but it was sad to think it had gone out like a little star in the morning light after a cold dark night of suffering.   And all owing to her neglect.

Geoffrey felt so sorry for her that he did not reproach her ; and after all, as he said, he had the funny, selfish Mrs. Mannikin left.

Uncle Arthur promised to try and get another mate for her, who might suit her better, and in the meanwhile she seemed very cheerful and contented. She hopped up and down, ate and drank, chirped and climbed, just as if nothing had happened. " She certainly is not an affectionate bird," said Fée. " If I were to lose Hugh I am sure I could not eat.   Mother, do you know that his bedclothes often slip off? and one night he could not get them back for ever so long.   Fancy, if he had died!"

" He might have got cold," said Geoffrey, " but he was not very likely to die, for he is accustomed to England and cold.   It would be a bad thing for me if my bedclothes came off, on account of my rheumy." He never could say rheumatism, though he was rather proud of his complaint, for he thought it was so grown-up to be rheumatic.   As he had to be ill, it was really grander to have a thing that grown-up people had, particularly as he got better, and was able to enjoy the grandeur without the pain.

"Amie is always very careful about tucking me well up, I must say.   She did not even forget last night."

There was an implied reproof in this remark which was rather painful to Eleanor, but she felt that she deserved it, and did not resent it.   She had been trying to explain to Geoffrey what sins of omission were, and he whispered to Fée when the elders had left the children to their own devices, "Perhaps Amie forgot to cover the birds so as to make me understand what a sin of omission is like."

Eleanor looked quite sad as she left the room, but Lilian comforted her a little by assuring her that poor Mr. Mannikin would very likely have died if he had been covered up. She had noticed that he had looked ill for some days, and he had never been a really thriving bird, like his little shrewish mate.

CHAPTER XXI.

MRS. MANNIKIN ALONE.

GEOFFREY was none the worse either for his bird's death or for the excitement of the concert. Indeed, every day brought more strength, and the doctor proposed, one bright December day, that he should go out on the terrace for ten minutes. He was wrapped up till he looked like a mummy: he had fur gloves and boots, and such a thick fur coat and cap, with ear pieces. He laughed at the idea of going out in such mufflings. " I feel much more *in* than out," he said ; but he was in tearing spirits, and made no objections. He found he could run better than he expected, though he looked like a curious ball rolling up and down the terrace, rather than the fairy with the butterfly motions, who had been the life and joy of the place during all the past summer until illness had overtaken him. Hugh and Fée met him, and each taking a hand of their long confined playmate, they helped him along. The ten minutes were over all too soon, but the children, in spite of their high spirits, were admirably trained in habits of obedience. There was no tiresome pleading for just one run more, no pouting, no loitering. They knew that the utmost time had been

given, that privations as well as pleasures were for their
good, and this ten minutes had been very delightful.
When Amie took off his wraps herself, she was rewarded
by finding two really rosy cheeks under the fur ear-pieces.
Geoffrey had naturally lost his bright colour during his
long illness and longer imprisonment, but there were his
flags, as he called those rosy cheeks, come out of their
cupboard. " I wonder exactly where they can be kept,"
he said, surveying them complacently.

" They are kisses from the fresh air. The sun and
the breeze add touches, and paint the cheeks of the
children they love," said Amie, fondly.

" How they must love you !" said Geoffrey, "they give
you such lovely pink kisses."

"I am very fond of them, and I am always in their
company," was Eleanor's gay reply ; " it would be hard
if we did not understand each other."

The French lesson went off all the more brightly after
Geoffrey's first interchange of greetings with the open
air, and then he did what he called Latin with uncle
Arthur. He perhaps learned as much as was good for
him at present of that dead language, but Amie used to
hear a great deal of conversation in the living mother
tongue as well. Perhaps a declension would be got
through ; indeed, that might or might not be the case, and
the word to be declined suggested a leading question.
That was all very well and instructive, but this word led
on to a further discussion, and perhaps the Latin lesson
proper began and ended with one declension. But then
the conversation was improving, Geoffrey was always

13

eager for real useful information, and as for uncle Arthur
the merry little boy did not know how much of the improvement he had noticed was due to his young com-
panionship and to these Latin lessons. Mr. Norman's
improvement was going to be put to a severe test. It
was wonderful how well he had borne the intercourse
with his former love and her husband. The contemplation of her happiness had rather taken from than
added to his bitterness. He was kind to the children,
friendly with her husband, and, after the first, easy and
natural with Lilian herself. He had braced himself up for
the year, and though what had been a trial soon became a
daily pleasure, still it was another matter when it became
a question of making a neighbour for life, by his own
act, of the woman he had wished to make his wife. It
happened on this wise : Mr. Russell, who held a canonry
in the cathedral town hard by, as well as the fat living
which was in the gift of the Normans, thought that at his
age, already nearly threescore years and ten, he might
give up the living in favour of a younger worker in the
Church's vineyard. He loved his residence in the dear
old minster yard, and he was hale and hearty still;
besides, he would have no say in the matter of his successor to the stall, but in the case of the living courtesy
at least would compel Mr. Norman to listen to his suggestions in the matter of a successor in the rectory. Mr.
Russell had heard of all the improvements in Arthur's
state of mind, as demonstrated by his more genial acts,
and gave the Chamberlaynes some credit for the happy
change. Arthur got Mr. Russell's letter by the second

post one December afternoon, soon after the concert, and he went to find Eleanor and impart the startling news to her. She was sitting between Geoffrey and the now solitary Mrs. Mannikin, and Arthur saw she was busy with their pet, so he sat down in one corner of the quaintly shaped room to wait till what seemed like a scéance was over. Six months ago Arthur would not have waited in this pleasant way. He would either have gone away without the consultation, or he would have disturbed Eleanor on the spot.

Mrs. Mannikin was talking to Geoffrey.

"And so the poor little brother did try what dying was like. I miss him more than I expected, especially during the nights. I am not so cold, but it is lonely and dark —for such a long time; and unless I happen to go to bed in the seed-place I cannot find it for certain in the dark, and I often get hungry. Poor little fellow, he was hungry that last night, and I actually fetched him some seed by feeling for it, and I tried to make him eat it, though I wanted it myself. But he said he dared not eat unless he were sure of getting a drink after; indeed, he thought it was drink he wanted more than food. He was very patient, and 1 knew he was suffering. I let him nestle up to me, though he made me feel quite cold and uncomfortable, he was so cold himself. It got light sooner than usual, for there was nothing over our cage, and when the fire began to crackle and to flicker on our cage I looked at my poor brother. His feathers were all inside out, his eyes were dim, and though I got him up to the water he could not drink. When the fire had

13*

warmed the room he looked better for a short time, and
thanked me for my kindness. I wished then I had been
kinder to him always; I wish it more than ever now.
I can only hope he is happier dead than he was
living. I should very much like to have my dear mate
with me, I should do everything in my power to make
him happy. I think he would be better off here than in
the dark shop where I left him. I only hope he has not
got another mate. I have got so used to my little cage
that I should not care to be in the little forest where my
mother is. I scarcely think I should care now to go
back to the real forest, if I had to take that terrible
journey to get there. I think if I could go to sleep on
one of these long dark nights, and wake up in the warm
light home of sun and heat, I should be almost too happy.
I wonder if death is the short way home? If my brother
is in our forest he is well compensated for all his
troubles. But these things puzzle me. I should like my
own mate."

Mrs. Mannikin slid down into the seed-place, but she
took her meal pensively, cracking each seed deliberately,
and looking round now at Amie and now at Geoffrey for
sympathy.

Arthur came forward when Amie rose from her chair,
and put Mr. Russell's letter into her hand. Her feelings
after reading it were very mixed, and she entered into her
brother's feelings at once, without speaking about them,
in a way that went far to balance and control them. She
did not allude in words to that part of the subject at all;
but after giving herself and her brother a cup of tea, and

attending to Geoffrey's wants, she said, "Will you go to the shop where you get these birds, Arthur, and try to get a mate for this poor little widow?" And she pointed to the cage where Mrs. Mannikin, in her widow's dress of black, relieved with white, was drinking, by dipping her funny little bill into the water, and then "straightway lifting up to heaven her head," as quaint old Herbert has it, suggesting that the bird is obliged to render homage to heaven for the blessed water even while it swallows it.

"Why not give it to the black bird in the aviary?"

"Why, they are a pair," said Geoffrey, with funna emphasis.

"So they are," said Arthur, laying a laughing stress on the plural pronoun.

"And I hope you will get its own mate," continued Geoffrey, eagerly, quite forgetting that he was betraying his own secret.

However, Arthur did not suspect anything, and only said, "I hope I shall be able to find a solitary cock—as you are pleased to call this lonely person *Mrs.* Mannikin."

"I suppose you would not like to go to Natalie for a little bit?" suggested Eleanor.

"You want to get rid of me," said Geoffrey, in a rather aggrieved voice. "Well, as it happens, I have something to do with Natalie. She is telling me a story, and, though it is in French, it is awfully amusing. It is about a knight Natalie calls Evanhoë, and his lady-love Rowena, and a Jewish lady called the same name as Isaac's wife in the Bible—Rebecca. The knight and the lady-love and most of the people are English, Saxon, but Natalie says they talked French always then, if they wished to be considered *du beau monde.*"

And Geoffrey ran away to follow Ivanhoe through his adventures, interpreted from the immortal Scott by romance-loving Natalie into her native tongue.

"Dear Arthur," said Eleanor, when Geoffrey had left them, "it will be a great trial parting with the Russells. But I daresay they will often pay us long visits, and Mr. Chamberlayne will be a worthy successor."

She took the succession as a matter of course, and her true rare tact saved both from any discussion of that part of the subject.

"After all it is pleasanter to see him resign after his long ministry than to part with him by the inevitable alternative which so often removes our nearest and dearest. It is a gentle way of stretching the silver cord that unites us, loosening it by degrees. Ask them to come and stay here when they return from abroad, before they go into residence."

And so Arthur wrote, accepting Mr. Russell's resignation regretfully, and his proposed successor cordially. Eleanor wrote to Mrs. Russell to say how nice Arthur had been about it all, and seconding her brother's invitation, which was gladly accepted by the charming old couple. The Chamberlaynes were not to be told of the good fortune in store for them until the arrival of the Russells, as these kind friends wished to be present when the living was offered. Lilian had grown quite robust, and the children were blooming. They were quite prepared to undertake any work that should offer; grateful for the refreshing country life, sorry to give it up and to part with their kind friends, but thankful for past good, and ready to find good in whatever the future might have in store.

They were the sort of people who deserved prosperity, because they were cheerful in adversity.

The two ladies are together in the rectory drawing-room, making arrangements for Christmas festivities, Christmas hymns, and Church decorations.

"Amie dear, how I shall miss you during the last months of my stay here ! It will make my departure less unendurable, however," said Lilian.

Eleanor smiled, though she spoke almost sadly. "I don't look forward to my Italian trip, *cara mia*, not even for the sake of the scenery, or the improvement of my Italian. I wonder if I shall catch the true accent of the *lingua Toscana* from the *bocca Romana*? I know very little of Italian, and Arthur knows less. Natalie says she speaks it, so we have decided to travel without a courier. But I see Natalie studying a book of dialogues, French on one side, and Italian on the other, and have doubts about her efficiency as an interpreter. However, we shall soon meet Mr. Gordon, and then our troubles on that score will be at an end. I have never been abroad, and, as I think Arthur rather looks forward to the trip, I try to cultivate pleasurable anticipations."

"You are sure to realise something pleasant. You cannot help being happy wherever you are. You are so essential to the happiness of those about you, and you are conscious of the duty you owe them on that score.

You are a very sunshine in a shady place, while in the light you hold your own and outshine all other brightness."

"Flatterer or 'wheedler,' as the heavy father says in the play. Well we have Christmas to look forward to before Italy, and the visit from the dear Russells, and I will not look on further for the present."

CHAPTER XXII.

MRS. MANNIKIN HAPPY.

"Where is our best Amie?" said uncle Arthur, coming into the sitting-room, to find Geoffrey rather lonely. In fact he was quite alone, and though some people are less lonely alone than in company, Geoffrey was not one of that sort. He was a thoroughly sociable little fellow. Christmas was drawing very near and Eleanor was overflowing with business, and altogether mysterious.

"I believe she is with the fairies, uncle Arthur." And Geoffrey's voice was certainly aggrieved. "She knows I want to see a fairy, and I know they are helping her to do something that will surprise me very much. Do you know what it is?"

"Would you like to know what I have got?" said Mr. Norman, skilfully evading one question by asking another, "or will you wait till I show it you?"

"I should like to know what you have got very much, but of course I must wait till you show it me."

"Then I will not keep you waiting." And Arthur produced a little square box, with wires in front, in which sat a handsome little mannikin.

"Oh, uncle Arthur!" And then after a pause as expressive as the exclamation, " Thank you, thank you so much.   I wonder if it is the right one ? " he continued.

" The man assured me it was a cock," said uncle Arthur, not knowing that there was one cock in all the world for Mrs. Mannikin and for Geoffrey.

" We must wait till Amie comes before we put them together," said the little boy.

Meanwhile Mrs. Mannikin was in a state of the wildest excitement, jumping up and down, climbing up her cage wires with beak and claws, chirping, and occasionally refreshing herself with now a sip of water and anon a seed.   The bird in the box cage trilled out a tiny song in reply to Mrs. Mannikin's chirpings, suggestive also of great ecstasy, and Geoffrey could hardly control his excitement.

At this moment uncle Arthur was called away, and Amie came into the room, evidently in search of something.

" Amie dear, I do believe uncle Arthur has brought Mrs. M.'s own mate ! " almost screamed Geoffrey, in his wild glee.

" Whose mate ? where ? " said Eleanor, in an absent voice.   She was thinking of the requirements of her Christmas tree in general, and of a doll for Fée Chamberlayne in particular.

" See," said Geoffrey, laconically, and producing his box cage.

" A new mannikin," said Amie, quite as interested now as her nephew.   " Oh, I do hope it is a cock, and also *the* cock."

" I think it must be," said Geoffrey.   " They are both

so excited. But I would not put them together until you came. Uncle Arthur had to go away, but as he does not know the story we need not wait for him." And Geoffrey as he spoke brought the box cage close to the door of the pretty pagoda, where Mrs. Mannikin had always reigned supreme, and latterly in solitary state. Both birds tried to get out of their respective cages, making the while such pretty twitterings that both aunt and nephew were enchanted. Amie raised the wires of the box, and opened the door of the pagoda. The new comer gladly left his box. The door of the pagoda, a palace by comparison, was closed, and the birds were billing and twittering in the prettiest way possible Busy as she was, Eleanor fetched her pen and prepared to chronicle the scene.

"At last we meet," said Mrs. Mannikin, in soft tender accents. Geoffrey did not know the voice of his whilom shrewish friend.

"Better late than never," twittered the new comer. "And what a pleasant home you have got."

"Yes," answered Mrs. Mannikin, joyously; "instead of your building a nest for me in our forest, and asking me to lay my eggs in it, I bid you welcome to my palace, and I say what is mine is yours." Then the two little bills met again. Afterwards Mrs. Mannikin proceeded to inspect her long-lost friend.

"Why what has happened to your tail?" she said. Mr. Mannikin was in splendid plumage; there was no suggestion of moulting about his glossy coat and spotless waistcoat, but never a vestige of tail could he boast of.

"My mother and sister begged for a feather in remembrance of me when I left them," was the answer, and the man who caught me pulled out the remaining feathers. I had just got my new plumage, but I had not changed my tail fortunately, so that it will soon grow again. I have my head and my feet and all my body, which are yours," said the gallant bird. "I always think a tail is the part we can best dispense with."

"Some of our old gaudy friends in the forest could hardly say that," laughed Mrs. Mannikin; "the ones who were all tail and no body, to speak of."

"But what a bother such tails must be!"

Just then a discordant scream was heard, and the tiny birds saw a splendid peacock outside the window, spreading his many-eyed tail in the brief December sunshine.

"That is as fine as any bird I ever saw," said Mr. Mannikin.

"Yes, but did you ever hear such a hideous voice?" answered the little lady.

"Often, my dear, and so have you in our forest home. Don't you remember the monkeys and the hyenas and the parrots? They made more noise than that one scream, though it is certainly bad enough. But what is that?" For the cock cut-throat in the aviary hard by recognised a friend's voice, and trickled forth a little song of welcome. "Surely it is my old friend with the coral necklace, or one of his tribe!"

"It is himself and none other," answered Mrs. Mannikin. "He was one of my travelling companions in the ship, and we came here together."

So Mr. Mannikin chirruped back an answer which meant that he was very grateful for this tuneful greeting.

"But where is your mother?" asked the new comer.

"She is in the aviary; and my brother is dead. He never was well, and I am ashamed to say I was not very kind to him until the last night we spent together, when he suffered very much. He was put in a little box after he was dead, without any wires in front, and without any seed or water, and I wondered if he would get back to our forest that way."

Mr. Mannikin shook his wise little head, it was too deep a question for him to solve.

Geoffrey had suggested sending the poor dead mannikin to heaven by post in perfectly reverent simplicity.

"What a pretty place!" said the new comer, who was evidently of a cheerful and contented disposition.

"So every one says," answered Mrs. Mannikin. "I did not think much of it when I first came here. It could not compare with our forest, but it certainly is better than the place you have just come from."

"I should think so, indeed, or the ship either. I am sure I shall be very happy now." Then the two mannikins stood side by side on the edge of their seed-place, and Mrs. Mannikin was so busy picking out the tit-bits for her tailless mate that she would have actually forgotten herself if he had not on his part attended to her wants. Then he took a bath, which was doubtless necessary after his journey, and Amie could hardly tear herself away from Geoffrey and his mannikins. They were, as he said, so very interesting.

But now the Christmas-tree was crying out for her. The short December day was drawing to a close, and as Geoffrey was quite absorbed in the contemplation of the happiness of his old and new friends the aunt slipped away unnoticed. Uncle Arthur came back, and was quite as pleased as Geoffrey to find the birds had taken so kindly to each other.

"I think they must have known each other before," he suggested.

Geoffrey looked as if he could hardly heep the important clue to the mystery to himself, but he managed to hold his tongue, and Arthur was too busy watching the pretty funny ways of the birds to look at Geoffrey; who told Eleanor afterwards that he felt like the frog in Æsop's fable, who tried to swell itself out as big as the ox. "Only I didn't try, Amie; I only seemed to be swelling and swelling until I was afraid I should burst. And uncle Arthur really was very clever to think it out of his own head that the birds had known each other before. I was quite afraid he might understand what they were saying." But Arthur had not even a suspicion of the great secret, and he was quite as much surprised as Hugh and Fée were when Eleanor read the wonderful story to them. We must not anticipate, for the birds had a little more to say, though in bird life, as in children's and grown-up life, prosperity is less exciting than adversity.

"I should like to have been the Children in the New Forest," sighed Geoffrey one day. "I wish I had never known you and uncle Arthur, Amie, unless he had been Jacob, and you might have been Alice, you know."

Eleanor had just finished reading that thrilling book aloud, for the benefit of Geoffrey and the young Chamberlaynes.

"What fun it must have been," said Hugh. "While Amie was reading it I quite seemed to be doing all the things they did. I should have been Humphrey, Geoffrey."

"Yes, of course, because he was the youngest. Edward was master of the house after Jacob died, so that would be me."

"And I should have been Edith," said Fée. "Amie would have had to be a little younger for Alice, or we might have done without Alice, and she might be Patience. I think we will play at being those children, instead of the game we have invented. I am tired of that game."

There was a little cottage ornée in the grounds. It was built in imitation of the Petit Trianon in the Versailles Gardens, a cottage where the unfortunate Queen Marie Antoinette used to play at being rustic. It must have been a pleasant change to leave the hooped petticoats and the stiff ceremonial of court life, and to dress like a shepherdess, rise with the flowers and the birds, and go to bed with them.

A Mr. Norman, who had lived when Louis XVI. and Marie Antoinette were King and Queen of France, took his bride for a trip to Paris. She was a beautiful young girl, brought up in the strict seclusion of a country parsonage. The splendour of Normanhurst rather overwhelmed her. She discharged all the duties of her new position with simple grace; but she secretly pined for the happy days when she had dug her own little garden, milked the cow, and helped her mother to make cakes for the boys' tea. Mr. Norman was a good deal older than she was, but she loved him with all her heart, or she would not have left her happy home to go with him. It was not quite a case of the Lord of Burleigh and his peasant wife, for Mrs. Norman was as well-born as her husband; but she was no more used to pomp and state than the "cottage countess."

She did not care for the Palais Royale, nor for the smart clothes her husband bought for her in Paris. She gazed with loving admiration on the beautiful face of the French queen, when she was presented at a grand reception, but she could not remember how the queen was dressed, to the great indignation of her own smart abigail.

She remembered every detail of the queen's simple costume when she paid her a visit at the Petit Trianon. Marie Antoinette had been fascinated by the fresh beauty and simple manners of the young wife of the rich grave Englishman, who was in the Government at home, and who had been received with great honour by the quiet gentle King of France.

When Mr. Norman asked his wife what present she would chose to adorn her future home in England, which should specially remind her of her visit to Paris, she answered without hesitation,—

"Make me a 'Petit Trianon' in the grounds of Norman-hurst."

This 'Petit Trianon' had always been the delight of

succeeding generations. Eleanor and Marian Norman had called it their house, had decorated the parlour with their most precious treasures, and had given tea-parties there on every holiday.

Arthur had given it to Geoffrey for his own house, on the first day he was able to walk so far after his illness.

Here they could really be the children of the New Forest, and many a happy hour was spent there, acting again the scenes that Amie had read to them, and which their fresh young memories had retained. Natalie was the willing maid-of-all-work in this beautiful 'Petit Trianon,' which recalled her beloved Paris so vividly, and she kept it in the most perfect order, actually scrubbing the floors herself, as she firmly believed the beautiful queen had done in her own little cottage. Natalie was a staunch royalist, and she pitied her nation for its present kingless state, as much as she had rebelled against the imperial rule. Indeed, she would say, "Better one head crowned, even a usurper, than a republic directed by a foreigner." She could never forget that the President of France had British blood in his veins.

14

CHAPTER XXIII.

HOW THE MANNIKINS LIVED HAPPILY EVER AFTER.

MR. and Mrs. Russell are coming to spend Christmas at Normanhurst. They are expected to-day, and Eleanor is making their rooms comfortable for them, putting hothouse flowers in the vases, and pots of snowdrops and ferns in a jardinière in the window, determined that, whatever external beauties of scenery they may have enjoyed during their foreign tour, they shall not be able to say they have been as comfortable in a house since they left England. Besides, she loves them both dearly, and is determined to do them all honour.

Lord Langley, Arthur's cousin and old schoolfellow, had proposed to spend Christmas with the Normans. He wanted to introduce his children to his cousins, and Eleanor had privately informed him of the improved state of affairs, so he thought it a good opportunity to propose a visit. His father, Lord Seaton, was abroad, so there was no home party at the Castle this year. Lady Langley's brother and only near relation was staying with the Langleys. He was coming too, and Regy, and Herbert, and little May, the three Langley children, of course could not be left alone at Christmas time. Regy was about Geoffrey's age, Herbert a year younger, May could just run alone.

Everything is ready, and Geoffrey, in the wildest excitement of anticipation, has yet sufficient interest in his mannikins to wish to wind up the story, "and we will hope they will live happily now for ever so long," he said.

" I should like to hear what they will all say to each other in the aviary," said Amie. And suiting the action to the word, she carried the cage into the miniature African forest.

Geoffrey of course followed, and they sat down on two wire chairs near the perch where Eleanor hung the birds.

The other birds were so well used to these visits that they did not flutter at all, but as soon as they recognised the mannikins in the pretty green cage several of them darted at the little pagoda and settled upon it. At first there was such a twittering and chattering of recognition that it was not easy to hear what the mannikins said, but presently little Mrs. M.'s clear voice became audible.

She greeted first one old friend and then another; the cut-throat welcomed her with such a delightful song that she declared the nightingale could not surpass it, and Mr. Mannikin said he was jealous. He wasn't a bit really, he was proud of the reception his wife received, but Mrs. Cut-throat did seem to object, and pecked her poor mate rather severely. Mrs. Mannikin with great tact addressed her, and congratulated her on her beautiful plumage and her charming domain, "of which," said the wily little bird, "you are evidently the queen by election as well as by right."

14 *

"It is well enough," answered the appeased bird; "but when you remember our forest this is but a poky hole."

"True; but when you think of our confinement on board ship, and even if you compare it with our lowly abode, yours is a very pleasant spot. Not that we are discontented. Since I have recovered my mate, I am more than satisfied, I am intensely happy; and the days pass so quickly they are over only too soon. The nights are long and rather cold."

"We have an advantage over you in that respect. Though our nights are long, they are as warm as the day."

"Ah," sighed Mrs. Mannikin, "that *is* an advantage. But one cannot have everything."

Amie and Geoffrey exchanged looks, but they did not speak.

Mr. Mannikin spoke now. It was the first chance he had had, for the ladies had held their own after the cut-throat's song, and had silenced their polite mates.

"I think it would be very delightful to stay here. I should like to keep our little home with the door open, then we could leave it at will, exercise our wings, which would be very good for us, and retire here when we had taken our exercise and enjoyed intercourse with all." He bowed politely, and there was a general twitter of approval. He felt it was very desirable to have their private larder and cellar, for he knew that Mrs. Cut-throat and Mrs. Mannikin had not always got on when provisions were common property. Mrs. Mannikin, in spite of the publicity, billed him affectionately;

and Geoffrey at a sign from his aunt opened the door of the mannikin castle. The birds hopped down, and played for a few seconds on the floor to support their dignity, not wishing to show undue haste. Mr. Mannikin bowed and billed his wife to the opening, they perched side by side on the door edge for a few minutes, and then flew. It was like a butterfly's flight, joyous and fairy-like; indeed, Eleanor seemed to see one of those beings of the imagination seated between the outstretched wings guiding the birds to some remembered African plant. They hung hummingbird-wise over the delicate blossoms of an oleander, and Mr. Mannikin caught an insect, which he gallantly presented to his lady. It was fresh and juicy, and reminded her of a meal in her own forest. Then they had a light dessert out of the heart of a trumpet-flower, and the other birds fluttered round them, evidently doing the honours of the place.

"It is a very good ending, Amie," said Geoffrey, with a little stifled sigh. "They will never be my own any more, but then I am no longer a prisoner myself, and I shall be more and more out every day, so it would be selfish to keep the little mannikins prisoners when they can be so happy here. I don't think they could be really happier in their own forest. It was not cruel to keep them when I did not know how happy it would make them to be here. But now I do know it I could not put them back in their cage. Dear beautiful mannikins, never be frightened of me when I come to see you."

Amie went on writing, for she liked to record

Geoffrey's unselfishness in his own simple words, and he was so taken up watching his treasures that he almost forgot her presence.

"And you are all to go to meet the Russells," said Amie, when Geoffrey turned to her and remembered how many joys life had in store for him, which he should enjoy all the more for thinking of the joy he had given to two wee birds. Their story was finished, but their lives would begin afresh in the freedom of the mimic forest. The joy would not be very great perhaps, but it would be even, flowing along like the rippling course of the cut-throat's song; and Geoffrey could see his friends every day, and enjoy their pretty graceful motions—as eloquent for expressing their joy as any speech could be.

The Russells arrived quite early in the afternoon, and Geoffrey went out twice a day now. Eleanor thought in her secret heart that as far as he was concerned the foreign trip was quite unnecessary, but then she knew what pleasure it would give his father to have him, and she thought Arthur was certainly looking forward to the expedition.

The children set off to the station. The patient ass, which carried the two younger Chamberlaynes in panniers, was further weighted with Hugh astride on its back, facing as equestrians are accustomed to face, the same way as the animal faced. But Geoffrey was also astride with his face towards the tail. The effect was ludicrous in the extreme, but on Geoffrey's expressive countenance sat all the grave eagerness of anticipation. For a wonder he had not assumed this unusual position for fun. They were coming from the station because it would make them too late to go all the way, but there was every chance of the carriage which had gone to meet the Russells catching them up. "So I will sit with my face to the tail," said Geoffrey, with perfect gravity, "and then it will seem as if I were coming to meet them, and I shall catch the first sight of them. It is not selfish, Hugh, because you do not know them, and they would not know your jolly little face."

Presently the rumble of wheels set Geoffrey wriggling, and he slipped off and began running towards the carriage, but not before the Russells had enjoyed a good sight of his "jolly face" perched above the ·donkey's tail.

"Oh, I am so benighted to see you," said Geoffrey, scrambling into the carriage, and kissing his friends with great effusion. He brought in one of his favourite long words somewhat inappropriately.

"Do you know what 'benighted' means?" said Mr. Russell, after the kind old couple had returned his greeting with warmth.

"A great deal more than glad," answered Geoffrey, with promptitude.

"I am sure that is the state of the case," said kind Mrs. Russell; "don't tease him with definitions, John."

But "John" knew it would not tease him, and he said gravely, though there was a twinkle in his eyes, "You said you were 'benighted' to see us. Now that means overtaken by the night. I am sorry the sight of us should shorten the days, which are short enough in December."

" Delighted, I meant ; of course I knew," said Geoffrey, joining heartily in the laugh against himself.

"I conclude your companions on that cruelly overladen beast of burden are the young Chamberlaynes,' said Mr. Russell.

"Yes, but you know the lot of us are not heavy," explained Geoffrey, anxious to disclaim any suggestion of cruelty to animals.

"By the way you are an invalid," said Mrs. Russell; "you don't look much like one."

"Oh. I am quite conversent, thank you," he answered.

"If you had said conversational, I should have agreed with you, and if you mean convalescent, which means recovering, I should say you have passed that step, and may be pronounced recovered, or quite well."·

"Mr. Russell, you are a great tease," said Geoffrey, who seemed to enjoy the process, though at his own expense.

"And now for more greetings," said Mr. Russell, as they drove under the portico.

"Mrs. Chamberlayne, you owe me a doctor's bill," was his merry greeting to his friend's wife ; "you look like a dairy maid—blooming as a peony in buxom May."

This was so funny a comparison that everybody laughed. Lilian was so much more like her namesake flower, though country air had done a great deal for her, and had brought a tinge of delicate rose colour into her somewhat pale cheek, that a peony would have blushed at such a comparison.

"As to you Eleanor, you are the châtelaine *par excel-*

lence. Edward " — to Mr. Chamberlayne — " you are getting fat." This was by comparison, perhaps; Mr. Chamberlayne was less thin, even as Lilian was less pale, than when Mr. Russell had last seen him.

The kind old rector made no personal remark about Arthur, who was in truth the most changed of all, but he wrung his hand warmly, and Mrs. Russell kissed him as she had always done after or before a long parting.

" How have we done without you all this time?" sighed Eleanor, contentedly, as she led Mrs. Russell to her cosy room, leaving the three gentlemen together, while Lilian went to look after the children.

" Very well indeed, to judge by appearances. But now tell me about everything, because your letters, charming as they were, tantalised me. You took it for granted that I knew things I did not know."

So Eleanor told all the story of Arthur's finding his old love in Mrs. Chamberlayne, and how well he had borne it. " Indeed, it seems to have cured him," put in the interested auditor. And then Geoffrey's illness had to be described, and the prank that had led to it. After that they entered into school and parish matters with hearty enjoyment, and then Mrs. Russell gave a short sketch of their foreign adventures.

" And you have been unselfish, as usual, and have kept the good news from the Chamberlaynes until we could enjoy their pleasure with you and them."

" After all, my feelings on the subject are mixed ones," said Eleanor. " Dearly as I love my new friends, I have often missed you, and when I know that it is to be for good, or rather for bad, I shall miss you more."

"The change will be for good," said the old lady. "The old order changeth, giving place to new. We have done our best, but we are too old for work. Work is more wanted now than it used to be when we were young, and even middle aged. John and I are going downhill together, and it is very pleasant to give the young toilers a friendly push up. And now I am going to send you away that I may rest before dinner."

CHAPTER XXIV.

A PLEASANT SURPRISE.

THE party at dinner that night was a very cheerful one. The Russells had so much to tell of their foreign experiences that they kept up the conversation between them. The four stay-at-home people put in bright intelligent questions from time to time, and their faces expressed their interest keenly. Arthur and Mr. Russell were able to compare notes, for they had been over·nearly the same ground, and Amie was glad to hear from Mrs. Russell that she had really enjoyed herself from beginning to end.

" But tell me truly," said Eleanor, half-wistfully, half-mischievously, "which was your most delightful experience?"

"The present moment, undoubtedly. I have seen everything ; I have forgotten the trifling discomforts and *contretemps*, or only think of them with amusement ; I am in a delightful English house, and I have no housekeeping cares on my mind. But for all that, if I were to wake up to-morrow and find out my foreign tour to be merely a dream I would set out the day after in order to realise it. I am glad you are going abroad, Eleanor."

"So am I," said Lilian, "though it is very unselfish of me to say so."

• The ladies now leave the dining-room, but the gentle-men follow them very quickly. They have just been looking at sleeping Geoffrey and the Chamberlayne children, for the rectory party are staying at the Hall for Christmas.

Close as the two houses lie together, Eleanor does not see why they should run backwards and forwards on December nights when there is room and to spare in the great rambling Hall; and of course the children are delighted to stay altogether with their beloved Geoffrey. They are secretly rather afraid that the unknown cousins who are to arrive on the morrow may prove too attractive, even to the putting on one side of old friends. But they did not say this, only they were very glad to be on the spot when the strangers should arrive.

Eleanor and Lilian are busy at embroidery—that dainty, beautiful art which has lately reasserted its worthy empire. Mrs. Russell, who had been a cunning embroi-derer in her day, was greatly interested in the present work, though she dared not try her eyes by displaying her own skill. That could be proved by the rectory chairs, which were still fresh monuments of that skill, in spite of the lapse of thirty years. There had been no children at the rectory until the Chamberlayne children came, and they were never allowed to romp in the drawing-room; besides, the chairs had been covered except on grand occasions, when Eleanor, from her earliest girlhood, had removed the covers, and called the attention of strangers to their beauty. Now Mrs. Russell knitted her husband's socks in the evening, and did plain work by daylight, for her sight was very good still, and she was just at this moment turning a heel and counting and talking at the same time.

" My dear," said Mr. Russell, laying his hand on his wife's shoulder, " Mr. Chamberlayne has been giving an account of his stewardship, and it is so satisfactory that though I am going to decide that he may be no longer steward, it is because I am going to ask him to take my place for good."

Mrs. Russell laid her own hand over the hand that rested on her shoulder with such fondness, and held out the other to Lilian, who was so much overcome that she could not speak at first.

Arthur took Edward Chamberlayne's hand and wrung it warmly, saying, " It is my pleasant privilege to confirm Mr. Russell's words. He resigns the living in your favour, and, though I grieve to part with him and his wife, I am glad to welcome so worthy a substitute."

Then Mr. Russell explained the state of the case, and Mrs. Russell did public homage to Eleanor for keeping the secret from the Chamberlaynes until the old rector and his wife could be present to enjoy their surprise and gratitude. Lilian had glanced at Arthur, and his calm answering look, which seemed to promise life-long friendship, reassured her. Mr. Chamberlayne, when he thoroughly understood that Mr. Russell no longer felt equal to parish work, accepted the offer in the spirit in which it had been made.

Even Lilian never knew that it had cost Arthur anything to confirm the offer of the living.   And, indeed, the
battle had been worth fighting.   Arthur was much improved, as his nephew had said; nay, more, he was
improving every day.   Though he could never resume the
careless brightness of his boyhood, he was becoming cheerful in a better way, for it was a cheerfulness that would
not be affected by any trouble that only affected himself;
he was learning to find by experience, as his sister had
seemed to know naturally, that the best happiness on
earth is to be found in seeking others' happiness and con-
tributing to it by every means in one's power.

Six very happy people went to sleep under the Normanhurst roof that night, and it would be hard to say
which of the six offered up the most fervent thanks to
Heaven.   Doubtless Arthur Norman had the most to be
thankful for, where all were grateful.   With this last act he
had exorcised his evil spirit, and he had so ordered his
heart and life that it was not likely that any such enemy
. would ever again conquer that citadel.

Eleanor was always thankful.   Each finished day
seemed to end too happily, and to find her glad heart
overflowing with praise.   Prayer was no empty form
with Edward Chamberlayne and his wife; and the good
old couple, who, like the beneficent fairy, had worked
all this happiness, took no credit to themselves, but
thanked God for having sent Edward Chamberlayne into
their way.

It was arranged between Amie and Geoffrey that the
story of the mannikins should be read to Mr. and Mrs.

Russell, to the Chamberlaynes, and to uncle Arthur before the arrival of the strangers; and at the witching twilight hour, when Mrs. Mannikin had been wont to make her communications to the favoured pair, Amie read the result to these dear friends. They were quite as much interested, surprised, and delighted as Geoffrey expected, and when the story was over they went into the aviary with new interest in all the little denizens. "I always thought they were fairies," said the namesake of those mysterious beings.

"Now I understand why you were so emphatic about the *right* cock," said uncle Arthur.

The children had prepared their own little surprise for the elders. Geoffrey, who had inherited all the true Norman talent for music, had been learning the violin. Uncle Arthur, who played it very creditably himself, had given him a few lessons, and the boy's correct ear had enabled him to pick out some tunes. The Chamberlayne children had sweet voices, and they had learned one or two simple songs and a couple of hymns. Fée and Hugh, with the two-year-old boy between them, each holding one of the chubby hands, stood opposite Geoffrey, with large eager eyes fixed on the bow of his fiddle.

He began with a really masterly prelude, then waved his bow, and the children gave with great spirit the ballad, so dear to infant schools, which relates the adventures of a certain "Apple-tree Tommy."

It was the prettiest scene, the youngest of the trio taking the words and tune from the elder's lips, and just audible like a little echo, quite in tune. Geoffrey playing in the strictest time, his face following all the emotions of the song, and speaking as plainly as the words did.

No need to say the applause from the grown-up people was loud and hearty; and it had scarcely died away before Geoffrey suggested another strain, and without the slightest thought of incongruity the children began to sing,—

> Safe in the arms of Jesus,
> Safe on His gentle breast,

only they pronounced gentle, "gencle," in the most engaging way. The elders were so taken by surprise that they continued to smile, and Geoffrey looked up reprovingly and said, " This is a hymn," without stopping either accompaniment or singers, and the audience composed their faces, duly reminded of the solemnity of the piece. Indeed, Amie had something in her eyes before the hymn was over, and they did not twinkle as Geoffrey said they were in the habit of doing; and Mr. and Mrs. Russell were quite husky as they thanked the little singers and the orchestra for a great treat.

"Am I a whole orchestra?" said Geoffrey.

"You represent one," said Amie. "You are whole as far as you go; not, perhaps, a *full* orchestra, which is made up of various instruments."

And now wheels are heard, and Eleanor and Arthur go to the door to receive their cousins. Geoffrey follows, but at a respectful distance. He is a little shy of strange relations. Lord Langley gets out first and hurries into the hall, leaving his brother-in-law to attend to Lady Langley.

He wrung Arthur's hand, and kissed Eleanor warmly. He had never had any sisters of his own, and Marian and Eleanor had scarcely let him feel the want of them.

"I have taken a great liberty," he began, hastily. "You know my wife's half sister, or perhaps you don't know, that she married an Italian grandee. The marriage was not liked, but I believe she was very happy. She died a year ago, leaving an only child, about seventeen years old, in my wife's charge. Margarita has been brought up in her mother's faith, but she was devoted to her father, and refused to leave him. He has just gone on a voyage round the world, and this little maiden arrived at our house yesterday quite unexpectedly. We could not leave her to spend a lonely Christmas, we could not give up the pleasure of coming to you, so we have brought her."

"You did quite right," said Arthur, stiffly but kindly.

"I should have given you no welcome at all," said Eleanor, "if you had left a foreigner alone at Christmas time. And this is Mary," as Lady Langley came forward. "You are not much changed." They had been friends as girls, and Eleanor had been Mary Merrivale's bridesmaid. They had never met since then, and the brother, Lord Merrivale, was quite a stranger. He was grave and shy, but decidedly good-looking. His sister Mary had the most charming face in the world, without any claim to actual beauty. Geoffrey described her best. "She looks so comfortable." He mastered the difficulties of the long word, and described the lady at the same moment. The children were real English

15

cherubs, with pleasant easy manners, and Geoffrey cousined with them at once. But every one paled beside Margarita, the little Anglo-Italian. She had taken the best from both parents, her golden hair and fair skin formed a wonderful but exquisite contrast to her liquid dark eyes and darker lashes and brows. She was like a fire-fly or a humming-bird, so slight, so fairy-like, so sparkling. Eleanor fell in love with her on the spot, and Geoffrey declared at once that he would marry her.

His beauty alone of all that goodly gathering was not eclipsed. He and Margarita set each other off, and they took to each other at once.

"I wish the elder Geoffrey were here," said Eleanor to her brother, as he came to her for the tea-cups, and she directed his attention to the two lovely heads in such becoming proximity. Lilian saw something in the expression of Arthur's face that made her smile, and before the evening was over it was decided that all the new comers were great and pleasant additions. This little southern bird could sing like the nightingale. Eleanor's organ-playing entranced her, and she begged her to let her sing some of the grand sacred music that requires the sustained accompaniment of the organ to do it justice. Her voice rose and fell, and filled the hall even when she only seemed to whisper, and the strains of " I know that my Redeemer liveth," brought an eager crowd to the open door. The servants were always allowed to fill the gallery whenever music went on, and some little bare-footed, white-robed angels suddenly glided into the

room. Lilian's children were awakened by the grand
swelling chords, and they had taken advantage of the
nurse's absence to slip out of bed and appear on the
scene. Little two-year-old had lisped out, "Don't go to
heaven without me!" for the children all thought such
music must come straight from the skies, so Hugh and
Fée helped him out of his crib, and brought him between
them. Geoffrey was awake too, but faithful to his
promise of not getting up without leave he contented
himself with shouting at the top of his voice, and Amie
heard him in a pause of the music, and rushed off to
see what was the matter.

"Oh, Amie, I heard the angels singing, and the music
came from the hall, and I have been so good, and didn't
get up because I promised not."

The house was well warmed, and Amie wanted to
reward her little boy. So she wrapped him in a soft
thick white Indian shawl, and carried him to the music-
room. Lilian had meanwhile fetched dressing-gowns
and slippers for her own trio, and though she shook her
head she smiled as Eleanor appeared with her white
fluffy-looking burden. Motherly Mary Langley held out
her arms for Geoffrey; and once more those delicious
strains stirred the hearts of all present. No one wished
to sing after Margarita, and the children had been
excited enough for one night.

"I suppose she will be an archangel in heaven," said
Geoffrey, as he settled his head on the pillow, to dream
of his mother singing on the step of a great white throne,
while he played on a golden violin.

15 *

CHAPTER XXV.

CHRISTMAS REJOICINGS.

THE elders of the party were as wakeful as the children that night. After Geoffrey had fallen asleep his faithful Amie remained at her favourite post by his bedside until a touch on her shoulder made her look up. Arthur was standing by her, gazing with almost fatherly devotion on the sleeping boy. She rose from her knees and he followed her into her bedroom. In old times the two sisters and this only brother had often chatted over the bedroom fire of one or other of the sisters till the small hours, but since Marian's marriage Arthur had given up the practice. Indeed, he and Eleanor had the whole day to spend together, and during what may be called the morose period of Arthur's life he never sought to exchange nocturnal confidences with Eleanor.

He seemed bright and cheerful to-night, and Eleanor drew her best chair close to the fire for his use and sat down near him on Geoffrey's chair.

"How pleasant it is," she began. "But, Arthur, I'm in love, there's no denying, love as deep as love can be—and with a girl ! That little Margarita has stolen the heart out of me, and as for Geoffrey, his poor old Amie will have to become number two."

"She is very lovely," assented Arthur.

"And how pleasant they all are," continued Eleanor. "Langley and Mary, and even quiet Lord Merrivale."

They talked on for some time, discussing plans, until it got so late at night, or rather so early in the morning, that Eleanor fairly drove her brother away.

Meanwhile "quiet Lord Merrivale" was raving in *his* sister's room about bonnie Eleanor.

Mary was teasing him, delighted all the same by his appreciation of the chosen friend of her girlhood.

"Ah, uncle Merrivale," says Margarita, who had stolen into her aunt's room, "you said you would never rave about any one but me!" She spoke the purest English, rather slowly and carefully in her speaking voice, which was as tuneful as her singing voice.

The fact was her uncle had been dazzled and bewitched by this little fire-fly like every one else. She was quite as much fascinated with Eleanor as Eleanor was with her, but she thought it great fun to tease kind, grave uncle Merrivale. She knew he would explain to her so gravely that his admiration for Miss Norman did not interfere with his devotion to his niece, and she was not disappointed of the explanation she had wilfully provoked. "And how grandly she plays the organ," said Lord Langley, quietly. "She does not get her musical talent from our side of the family."

"No, she inherits that from the Normans. No doubt there is troubadour blood in their veins : their ancestors

came over with the Conqueror, and before that they may
have come from smiling, singing Provence."

"How like Mary to dive into the dark ages to explain
Eleanor's enlightened playing," laughed her husband, who
loved to tease his somewhat matter-of-fact wife when she
aired her reasons and her learning. She always took such
teasings in good part, and now Margarita's sweet voice
changed the subject.

"I like that lovely boy's name for her—Amie. I
shall call her Amie; I should like to call the boy Angelo.
He is like an angel."

"A very human one I should say," was quiet but
observant Lord Merrivale's remark. "Did you hear him
shouting to come to the music-room?"

"Yes; but did you hear, uncle, how angelic he was
about that? He had promised not to get out of bed
without leave, and he thought the angels were singing,
and he wanted to see them."

"You vain puss! Angels, indeed! All of a sort you
and he. I suspect if you two enter into an alliance offen-
sive and defensive a great many promises will have to be
extracted from angel Geoffrey if he is to be kept out of
mischief. And now go to bed, you will have no beauty-
sleep as it is." And uncle Merrivale sent Margarita to
bed and took himself off at the same time.

Lord and Lady Langley must have had something very
interesting to discuss, Margarita heard the murmur of
their voices until she fell asleep in her room hard by, but
they would not tell her what the talk had been about,
though she tried hard to find out next morning.

"I like the grave, kind signor—squire they call him," was the little humming-bird's last waking thought.

"Christmas Eve, Geoffrey, and you are still asleep." And Amie stood over her sleeping cherub, fresh and fair and smiling in the crisp frosty sunlight of the December morning.

"Hark, the herald angels sing," he murmured, and his bright eyes opened, and Amie was nearly smothered and very much tumbled by his morning greeting.

"I was dreaming that I saw the shepherds in the sky, and the angels keeping watch over their flock by night; and it was all lighted up by a burning bush."

It was a strange combination of Old and New Testament history, with a little confusion and displacement of persons. But Amié understood him, and told him the beautiful story over again, of the lowly shepherds who were first privileged to hear the good tidings of great joy. The burning bush out of which God talked to Moses was typical of the bright light that was to illumine the Christian world; but there was a great deal to accomplish before these humble descendants of the children of Israel were to see the angels who announced the actual birth of Christ—this great company of the heavenly host praising God and saying, "Glory to God in the highest, and on earth peace, goodwill to men."

"I like the story of the shepherds almost better than the one about the wise men," said Geoffrey, as Eleanor settled his little rose-coloured tie and kissed his bright face, all glowing after his morning ablutions. "The gold they offered and all their grandeur could not have been so grand as the angels which were seen by the poor shepherds. I should like to have been one of those shepherds."

" You are better off as a little English Christian boy," said Amie ; and then he ran away to join his old friends and his new ones.

The children spent a very happy day, though they saw scarcely anything of their elders, who were generally very conducive to their gladness and merriment. It is so well for grown-up people and children to be essential to each other ; it is as good for the elders as for the small people. It keeps sympathy fresh, and it is such a blessing for people, as they leave youth behind them, to live it over again in their intercourse with the young ones who are treading in their footsteps. But on this occasion the children knew the elders were preparing something for them, and they were brought up to be able to amuse themselves. Besides, Margarita devoted herself to them for the chief part of the time, though she was occasionally summoned in a mysterious way.

"You see, the fact is," said Geoffrey, solemnly, "the fairies are helping, and I suppose Margarita has something particular to do with them. I should not be at all surprised to hear that she has a fairy godmother. I never saw any one so beautiful except in a fairy tale, where the princess has a fairy godmother."

" Did you ever see *in* a fairy tale ?" asked his cousin Regy, quite eagerly.

"Oh yes," was the grave answer. "I see it all while Amie reads it to me. I generally half-shut my eyes, but I *can* see with them either open wide or quite shut. Fée sees the things, too, but Hugh can't. Amie says it is because he is mattery fac."

"I am afraid I am that, too," sighed Regy, not venturing on the pronunciation of the remarkable affliction which prevented a fellow from seeing a thing that was not visible to ordinary eyes, and which, being pronounced quite accurately, would be "matter of fact," which means that a person can only see things that are facts or realities.

"Pearl," said Regy, suddenly—the children preferred the English rendering of their Anglo-Italian cousin's pretty name—"what do you see when you are singing?"

"What I am singing about," she answered, laconically.

"Ah, then, you are like Geoffrey. You see things inside your head, and in the lining of your eyes, instead of outside, as Hugh and I do."

And now it is getting dark, and there are sounds of arrivals. There is to be a Christmas party. The neighbours are bidden to the Christmas-tree, which is to be the surprise of the evening, and they are being ushered into the small withdrawing-room, in the public suite of rooms. The yule-log is already crackling in the great banqueting-hall, where children and grown-up people are to have a sort of general meal. The mystery will be developed in the great withdrawing-room. Marguerite is now called away, and the children are in an agony of expectation.

"Do you think we shall see the fairies?" said little Fée, not realising how fairy-like she looked herself.

"Mother," as Lilian came towards them smiling, "have you kept the fairies?"

"Come and see," was the answer; and out of the gloom of the unlighted banqueting-hall, where the company had been mustered, burst through the great folding-doors which led into the withdrawing-room, that miracle of grace and light and beauty—a gigantic Christmas-tree!

It was so brilliant and so dazzling, that it was difficult at first to decide what it was. Geoffrey distinctly saw a flight of fairies, and Fée caught a glimpse of them as they disappeared, revealing to the now accustomed eyes the full glory of the lighted tapers, which were reproduced in a thousand different sconces.

"It is a wonderful tree, with lights for flowers, and gold and silver fruit, and presents for everybody, I am sure. Thank you, dear dear fairies," said Geoffrey, squeezing his hands tightly together, as was his habit when strongly moved.

"Ith it heaven, mover?" asked Lilian's solemn two-year-old son, with one arm round her neck and the other pointed towards the glittering marvel.

"It is a Christmas-tree," explained Regy Langley, who had enjoyed one on a smaller scale the year before. Geoffrey had never seen one; the few Christmases he could remember, perhaps two at most, had been spent at a house where the presents were mysteriously cooked in a bran box or pie. It was great fun finding them, but it was far more delightful seeing them in such beauty. It was hard to say what was prettiest to-night, the tree, or the children's gracious unfeigned delight, or the calm sweet complaisance of the elders. Perhaps the combination was almost perfect, and Amie felt so happy she very nearly cried, and had to busy herself suddenly with a tipsy taper, which so overrated its own consequence, that it fell to one side and nearly set a lovely doll on fire, which was spinning round like an opera dancer, thanks to an invisible elastic, which made her appear to be supported only by her gauzy wings. The tree furnished ever-varying delight for an hour; every moment fresh beauties were discovered, and after that time, while the lights burned lower, the elders distributed the presents. Eleanor thought Lord Merrivale was the most useful man in the world on such an occasion. He knew every one in the room, and found the right presents, when she herself, in spite of her method and order, got bewildered. Arthur on the other hand tried to demoralise Margarita by engaging her in conversation, but she said decidedly, "I belong to the children to-night, and so do you, grave signor; we grown-up people"—she was just seventeen—"must reserve our interests for discussion by-and-by."

Mr. and Mrs. Russell were undoubtedly the youngest people present. They were as happy as the children, as active as the young men and women, and, in a word, the life of a party where all were lively. The supper was scarcely less delightful in its way, and the popping of crackers, the ripple of laughter, the unceasing flow of conversation, made it worthy of a foreign scene.

"I thought the English were always 'triste,' sad, when they took their pleasure," said Margarita, who was now rewarding "Signor Arturo" by talking to him during supper; "I assure you we are not more merry in Italy than you all are."

"It is your influence," said Arthur, speaking truthfully as far as he was concerned.

"You are flattering me. I am very happy and very glad; but the scene would be as bright, as happy, as glad, without me."

Very likely this would have been the case, but no doubt this bright fire-fly, as those English people loved to call Margarita, then and always, shed a bright ray across Arthur's plate while he eat his supper. After supper there were games, and the children kept awake till twelve o'clock, when the great hall doors were thrown open, and the squire himself held on high the remains of the great yule-log, or rather a goodly splinter separated from the main log, to light Father Christmas out of the cold dark night into the hospitable halls of mirth and light. And after this social rite had been performed, the merry party exchanged Christmas and Christian greetings, and separated for the night.

CHAPTER XXVI.

CHANGES AGAIN.

CHRISTMAS DAY was beautiful. There had been a slight fall of snow in the night, making the trees look like maiden brides, and lying soft and white on the face of the earth. The frost had been pretty sharp in the early morning, so that the snow was crisp and dry for walking. The sky was cloudless, and the brave robins sang gay roundelays to greet the morn when Christ became a child. Amie was explaining to Geoffrey how the great King of heaven and earth, the Lord of lords, the only Son of His Father, had become a little helpless babe on this day, to save all mankind from the dreadful fate that the first man had prepared by his sin for the whole of the unborn future generations of the world.

"How could a great King become a baby?" asked Geoffrey. "I could not become a baby, and I am not a very big boy yet."

"No human being could have done it, it was brought about by Almighty power. First He became a little help- less babe, tended and cared-for by His loving mother. But she was very poor, she could only wrap this holy

Infant in the coarsest of swaddling clothes. She had no lovely cradle like the one your little cousin May lies in; when she wanted to rest herself she was obliged to lay this precious Child in a rude manger in the stable where He was born."

" What is a manger? "

" The rack where the hay is put for the animals to eat. You remember there was no room at the inn for these poor travellers when they arrived. Mary was no doubt feeling ill after such a long journey, and Joseph, her husband, must have been footsore and weary. Both these people were descended from King David in the direct line, but the Jewish nation was no longer a kingdom. Their country was in the hands of the Romans, the conquerors of the then known world, and the descendants of the ancient kings of Judea were obliged to toil for their daily bread. Joseph, the husband of Mary, was a carpenter; our blessed Saviour followed the same trade."

" Oh, Amie, did our Saviour make things just like our carpenter does here, and do you think He mended things for little boys just as Harper does? "

" Doubtless He did. You remember how He loved the little children, and how He brought them forward after He had begun His public ministry. During the thirty years which He spent in retirement, of which we have no record whatever, we can picture to ourselves many a gracious deed performed in secret, as from man to man, and accepted as a matter of course."

" Oh, if they had only known!" said enthusiastic

Geoffrey. "Fancy if He had mended something for me! How I should have loved it!"

"Perhaps you might have loved it too much. You might have prized a senseless thing to the extent of almost forgetting what first made you value it, and sweet and gracious as our Saviour must have been in private as in public life, none of His acts encourage us to dream or sentimentalise. If we would follow Him we must work hard, not only doing whatever our hands find to do, well, but looking about, seeking how we may further benefit others, remembering that if we do it unto the very least of our fellow-creatures, Christ Himself has said we do it unto Him."

Geoffrey joined his young companions after this conversation, looking as bright and joyous as usual. But Eleanor noticed that he took more pains than was even his wont to make everybody happy. Fond as he was of his young friends, he would have preferred attaching himself, Amie knew, to Margarita. But he seemed to know by instinct that uncle Arthur liked talking to her, and that the children enjoyed his undivided attentions, and so he gave himself up to them, while Margarita, with equal unselfishness, he thought, talked to uncle Arthur, instead of following her inclinations and joining the young ones.

The little humming-bird proved to the village generally, and to the choir in particular, that she could sing with the best of them.

After a very short joyous voluntary Mr. Chamberlayne gave out the favourite hymn, "Christians, awake," to the tune called Yorkshire, and Amie made the organ sing and shout with joy before ever the choir attempted to swell the glad strain.

Geoffrey had learned to be quite reverent in church, and when deár old Mr. Russell preached, as he did on this occasion, Geoffrey listened gravely, and gathered all the simple truths he could understand from the scholarly, old-fashioned discourse.

Margarita listened to the first verse of the introductory hymn and then joined in, leading unconsciously, somewhat to the consternation of the leading boy, whose musical instinct told him his voice was eclipsed. The boy next him, who was rather jealous of him, whispered, "Yon lady ought to have the solo," which put young Franks on his metal, and he astonished his teachers by the way in which he sung the solo in the anthem.

When the service was over Margarita waited behind for Eleanor and asked in her pretty manner,—

"May I tell that boy how well he sang?" And Franks blushed and quivered with delight, though when he joined the other boys he said nothing at first. Only when the next best boy asked him what the pretty lady had given him, he answered with pardonable triumph, "She told me I had sung the solo better than she could have sung it herself."

It would have been really impossible to have sung it better, and the choir-boys were properly proud of Franks, so that even his rival did not grudge him the well-deserved praise.

If Christmas Day was quieter in some ways than the

Eve had been, it was quite as happy, and the whole glad week slipped away all too quickly, bringing the young year to its birthday, and the merry party to the end of their union for the present.

But the Langleys, with Lord Merrivale and Margarita, were going to Italy, and Eleanor found out that she really was looking forward to her trip. It would be so pleasant, she thought, with Margarita to describe everything to her. Geoffrey was longing to see his father, and the marble mother, and uncle Arthur was in really high spirits at the Italian prospect.

Of course the parting with the Chamberlaynes was sad, especially for the quiet rectory party who had to stay at home—"But we shall soon be back again, and then it will be all the same, only jollier than ever."

It might be "jollier than ever," but would it ever be the same again?

Eleanor is in Rome, feeling, she says, very like *Joan* Bull—and a little home-sick, she thinks, but she keeps that to herself. She and Geoffrey are in Mr. Gordon's studio. He has left them to take their first look at his statue alone. Of course it was not nearly finished yet, though he had worked very hard. The figure, instead of being recumbent as usual, was standing in an easy natural position, and the little babe which had lived for nearly a fortnight was in her arms. The likeness was already marvellous. It was a labour of love, and the genius of the artist enhanced the effect of hard work. Indeed, the face was all but finished, the chief labour

16

now lay amongst the drapery. The child's head rested on her shoulder. In her disengaged hand she held a lily towards her daughter.

> Bear a lily in thy hand,
> Gates of brass cannot withstand
> One touch of that magic wand.

Heaven's golden gates had already rolled back when the mother had guided the childish hand towards the glittering portals armed with that spotless wand.

The babe held a few snowdrops on its little breast, the delicate flowers hung between the fingers, which hardly clasped the tender bells.

Amie stood smiling before the unfinished work, unconscious of her quickly falling tears.

Geoffrey neither cried nor spoke, but looked and looked as if he would fain imprint it on his brain.

"It is mother as I saw her last. Only she was lying down then, and she is standing up now. I suppose she can stand and fly and move as she pleases now, or father would not have made her like that. She could not move when I saw her last."

And then, Geoffrey's eyes overflowed as he recalled that sad, grave, still time, and his Amie thought he had been long enough in this fair but inanimate presence.

Mr. Gordon was in the pretty morning room, where Amie and Geoffrey joined him. He looked up brightly, and she said quietly, "It surpasses my expectations." "It is mother," added Geoffrey, softly; and Mr. Gordon kissed his boy, and clasped his sister's hand as it rested on his shoulder.

No more passed on the subject, and Mr. Gordon and Arthur gave themselves up to the enjoyment of showing Rome to the aunt and nephew. Eleanor enjoyed it very much, but there was a wistful look in her eyes sometimes, and Geoffrey used to say, " You are looking at Normanhurst, Amie, not at St. Peter's."

It was not quite that either, for after the Langley party joined them she saw everything with shining happy eyes. " The twinkling stars come back again without Normanhurst," said Geoffrey.

Uncle Arthur was boyishly happy, and Margarita gave up calling him the grave Signor Arturo. She had found out Natalie's name for him, and she addressed him one day as " Sir Boompkeen Squire," to the delight of every one, especially of Geoffrey and of the squire himself.

Mr. Gordon was very glad to renew his acquaintance with his wife's near relations, but after their arrival he used not to join the expeditions so frequently as before. He was very glad to be useful to his brother and sister-in-law, but now that they had guides who knew the lions as well as he did he was more than glad to resume his lately neglected labour of love. If Amie had found Lord Merrivale helpful and pleasant in a Christmas party, he was still more delightful as a travelling companion. He seemed to know exactly how much she enjoyed seeing; and she never now felt that a thing must be seen or done, as is often the case with conscientious tourists, but she felt she should really like to see it. Geoffrey was so perfectly well that it was decided that German waters would be quite unnecessary, and Eleanor breathed a sigh

16 *

of relief. " I did dread three weeks at a watering place,"
she confided to Lord Merrivale.

"I daresay Mary would have found out that Margarita was rheumatic, and we should have followed you wherever you went, the boompkeen squire could not have
done without some of us."

Lord Merrivale may have been quiet, but he was full
of fun, and Eleanor laughed heartily at the joke, which
had now become a very favourite one amongst the merry
party.   They made expeditions to Naples, to the lakes,
to Sicily, in spite of brigands, and time seemed to fly.

Geoffrey did begin to long for the Chamberlaynes
sometimes, although his Langley cousins were very delightful; but he was such an unselfish little fellow, and
he felt they must miss him very badly in the now deserted
gardens at Normanhurst.

However, April is drawing to a close, and it is too hot
to linger in Italy.   They are going home through
Switzerland, and Mr. Gordon gave himself a holiday in
order to accompany them.   The weather was delightful,
fresh, and still warm.   May flowers were fast coming out
in the sheltered Swiss valleys, while the mountain tops
gleamed against the rosy sky at sunset in their everlasting
crowns of snow.

"Do you like Switzerland as much as Italy?" asked
Arthur, as he and Margarita gazed at Mont Blanc.

" Italy is my fatherland," she answered.

" How tame and dull England must seem to you after
this," said Arthur, sadly.

" I spent the happiest time I ever remember in all

my life in England. Besides, it is my mother's country," exclaimed Margarita, speaking from her vantage height of seventeen years' experience, including babyhood.

"Could you live always in England?" asked Arthur; and that evening, blushing like the sunset itself, Margarita told Geoffrey he must call her his aunt in future.

CHAPTER XXVII.

"ALL'S WELL THAT ENDS WELL."

NORMANHURST is in great beauty. All the flowering shrubs are at their best. Laburnums rain down golden tears; lilacs, purple and white, scent the air; the hawthorns bend beneath their veils of snowy blossoms, and the chestnuts look like summer Christmas-trees.

The train from London stops at the little Hurst station, the indignant heads appear to know what has happened. Geoffrey Gordon, grown sunburnt and manly-looking— he is seven years old now—touches his hat with rustic courtesy, and explains that the train is stopping for him and his aunt to-day, but if they happen to be passing that way a few days hence it will stop for two no less important persons than Mr. and Mrs. Norman.

Yes, Margarita is Mrs. Norman. People who cared for rank and titles tried to call her Marchesa, for some such title was hers by right, and by long descent too, but she would have no name but Arthur's. Geoffrey's delight was beyond all bounds, but he was very saucy to his aunt-elect before she actually became Mrs. Norman.

"Call you aunt, you little fairy!" he said—she was considerably taller than he was—"why I don't even call

Amie aunt, and she does look like a queen. You are just like a humming-bird, little Margarita, pretty Pearl." And then the bride-elect made a hummingbird-like dart at the offender, but missed him, and the discussion ended in a merry chase and a romp; while the grave " Signor Arturo" stood looking on with a happy smile on his face.

They had been married in the middle of May, as soon as they reached England, at Lord Merrivale's beautiful place, and then Eleanor hurried home to see that all was right at Normanhurst.

Mr. and Mrs. Dene received her with tearful cordiality. Well-pleased at Mr. Arthur's marriage to the sweet half-foreign flower to whom they had already lost their hearts, but wondering how they could bear to see Miss Norman deposed from her well-fulfilled reign.

She was more joyous than ever, and her face looked so young and bright that Geoffrey said, " I daresay people take you for my big sister."

There were wild interchanges of endearments between the traveller and the Chamberlayne children; and Lilian was brimming over with gladness as she kissed Eleanor.

" Arthur wants me to stay and help Pearl," says Amie, quite ready to become Cinderella for those she loved.

" That will be charming," answers Lilian, with a roguish look in her eyes. " You will be a sort of lady housekeeper, I suppose. Normanhurst really requires one when the châtelaine is so young."

" Yes," answered Eleanor, simply, " and I am to keep

my own rooms, and Geoffrey is to stay with us, and when he goes to school there will perhaps be some successors to fill up my spare time."

"Always a sunshine in a shady place," said Lilian; "and, moreover, wilfully seeking the shade. Well, I cannot be jealous of Margarita even for your sake. She will make Arthur happy, and she will do her duty by his place and people."

There was a look in Eleanor's face that satisfied Lilian of a good prospect in store for her independently of Mr. and Mrs. Norman's happiness.

She asked no questions, however, until she got Geoffrey to herself, while her children were hearing details of the wedding from Amie.

"What sort of a place is Merrivale Castle?" she asked.

"A real grand castle, with a keep and a moat and a drawbridge," was Geoffrey's answer, with a great stress on the drawbridge. "There are such curious things—dungeons, secret chambers, and secret staircases. Amie dressed up one night in some old clothes that belonged to a Lady Merrivale who lived ever so long ago, and aunt Mary got some jewels from Lord Merrivale, and covered Amie with them till she shone like the sun. Amie looked at herself, and she was obliged to smile. She knew she looked like a queen or a—what do you call the lady of a castle?"

"Châtelaine?" suggested Lilian.

"Yes, that is the word. Then aunt Mary wanted her to come downstairs, but she said she would not come.

The room where the things are kept is the oldest in the castle.   It is done up with silver and blue, and furnished with such funny chairs and things.   Lord Merrivale came in while aunt Mary was teasing Amie to come down, and I think he must have taken Amie for the beautiful Lady Merrivale she was dressed like.   Of course you know he only knew Lady Merrivale by her picture, as she had been dead long before he was born.   But she was his relation, and if it had really been her he would have been very glad to see her, and I daresay he would have kissed her.   I really thought he was going to kiss Amie, he did look so fond of her."

"Do you like Lord Merrivale?" asked Lilian, much interested.

"Yes, I like him, and he is not so grave as we thought.   I know Amie likes him very much, so he must be nice."

After this Mrs. Chamberlayne asked no more questions, and the next few days were spent in preparing for the arrival of the bride and bridegroom.   The triumphal arches were so beautiful they looked like nature, the trees looked as if they had been dressed on purpose to greet a bride, the birds sang regular marriage lays, and excitement and expectation were on tip-toe.

The great day soon arrived, the cathedral bells crashed and clanged all day; one or two of the principal farmers, who were the proud possessors of dinner-bells to call the labourers to their meals, rang them incessantly to emulate the minster bells.   The church bells far and near took up the tale, for the whole country was glad to welcome a bride to Normanhurst.

Of course the tenants' sons assembled to draw the carriage from the station to the house, and the tenantry, mounted on their best horses, formed a gallant escort. The train was punctual to a minute, and for once the remaining passengers were not cross at the delay, for they were glad to have a good look at the decorations, the gay crowd, and, above all, the lovely smiling bride and the handsome happy-looking bridegroom. They had brought a large party with them, and there was to be a grand ball, besides several garden parties, a tenants' dinner and dance, school feasts, fireworks, and all sorts of rejoicings.

Lord Merrivale was gratified by noticing that even at this first reception of their future lady, and she such a winsome one, Eleanor was the object of the tenderest affection and the most devoted loyalty.

While every one strained their eyes to get the first look at the bride, many a glad proud glance bore witness to the charms of Miss Norman as she received her sister-in-law, and led her herself to the carriage. Side by side the princess-regent and the new queen received the greetings of the crowd.

"They will love me, Amie, because you show them that you love me," said the little humming-bird.

Geoffrey rode by the carriage on his proud Sheltie, with his bright curls uncovered, and his lovely eyes shining with delight. Arthur sat opposite his wife and sister, talking and laughing with the eager crowd with the same gracious freedom which was Eleanor's peculiar charm.

Geoffrey was anxious to interest Margarita in the aviary, and as soon as she had got over the first greetings, he dragged her off to make her a partner in the firm.

" Now they belong to you as well as to me and uncle Arthur and Amie."

. And Mrs. Norman was duly gratified by this share in the principal treasures, at least in Geoffrey's eyes, of Normanhurst. The mannikins had white satin ties round their necks in special honour of the occasion. Geoffrey had so adorned them early that morning, taking somewhat mean advantage of their retirement into their cage, where they always spent the night. However, they looked well and happy, and they had not seemed to mind the actual operation as much as might have been expected. They were in splendid plumage, and Mr. Mannikin's tail was fully grown. All the birds looked well, and the cut-throat sang his very best song to greet his new mistress.

It would take a whole book to describe all the entertainments which followed. Geoffrey was in hourly danger of bursting with happiness. It was wonderful how he kept out of mischief, but really there was so much to see and to do and to enjoy, he had no time to devise anything for himself. This may have accounted for his good-behaviour. Besides, he had to relieve Eleanor from Lord Merrivale's society, whenever he could take upon himself the arduous task of entertaining that particular guest.

" It must be a bore for her when she has so much to do, having the man following her about everywhere," he confided to Lilian one day. She, by the way, seemed as happy as any one, and whispered in Amie's ear, " How grateful Arthur ought to be to me !" To which Miss Norman replied, " All's well that ends well, and as everybody is satisfied, and I have Pearl for a sister, and you for a neighbour and friend, I do not wish for more."

A day or two before the party broke up, Geoffrey came to Lilian with very red cheeks. The festivities were at an end, but the Langleys and Lord Merrivale were still lingering, unable to tear themselves away.

" Do you know that Lord Merrivale has just kissed. Amie in the garden with the fountain, where I bathed last year ? He could not have taken her for any one but herself, she was just in her usual white dress. She did look very pretty, but he is no relation at all, and he ought not to have done it, ought he ? "

" What did Amie do ? " asked Lilian, gravely, but with a twinkle in her eyes.

" She seemed as if she liked it."

Before the summer was over there was a wedding at Normanhurst. Mr. Russell and Mr. Chamberlayne had the pleasant task of sharing the labours of uniting Lord Merrivale to Eleanor Norman, and the people forgave him for taking her away from Normanhurst, partly. because he was uncle to Mrs. Norman, who was trying so hard to do everything Miss Norman did, so that they might not miss her very much. Geoffrey would have cried during the whole wedding ceremony, only Lilian, who was near him, assured him he would make himself such a figure Amie would not kiss him before she went away, and that it was not manly to cry. There was a suspicious something in Lilian's own eyes, but she winked it away, and consoled herself with thinking how happy Lord Merrivale looked.

As for Amie, she felt like an April day, but she behaved like an August one, after the July rains have exhausted themselves and the best sort of harvest-weather has set in.

"All went merry as a marriage bell," and Geoffrey made up his mind that the next wedding in the old church should be celebrated between himself and Fée.

Meanwhile he was to spend the remainder of his bachelor life between Normanhurst and Merrivale Castle, and he actually consented to allow Amie to take her wedding trip without him.

"Pearl and I can get on very well," were his last reassuring words, as Eleanor Merrivale tried to smile as the carriage drove off.

"He is a lucky man," said one.

"And I think he deserves her," said another of the retainers, who knew well what she was worth.

"They that sow in tears shall reap in joy," and those who weep with the sorrowful, and rejoice in others' joys, do find their reward even in this life. Whatever happened in the future, Eleanor Merrivale would always be happy, because she sought and found her happiness in the happiness of others, and her husband was another of the same rare sort.

UNWIN BROTHERS,
PRINTERS,
CHILWORTH AND LONDON.

a moral. Moral and tale are blended together in an admirable manner. Kindness and humanity to the dumb creation (in Miss Milner's hands it is a very eloquent creation) are the lessons which are sought to be instilled. . . . There is a degree of literary excellence in the descriptions and incidents which would be an ornament to a more pretentious work."—*Scotsman.*

"This is a charming book. . . . The volume extends to 175 pages, and is beautifully got up. The wood-engraved illustrations (16 in number) were drawn by the Hon. Mrs. E. Stanhope, and their execution is highly creditable to the artistic talent of that lady." —*Yorkshire Gazette.*

"A series of enchanting child-stories, elegantly told, and full of happy suggestions. The letter-press, illustrations, and general appearance of the little work are admirable."—*Liverpool Albion.*

"The author certainly knows how to write for children, and has sufficiently studied the traditional manner of fairy speech to make the book no less characteristic than amusing."—*Manchester Examiner.*

"A rich fancy and a heart yearning with true womanly sympathy with all that is beautiful and gentle, and deserving of respect, reveal themselves in every page of this pleasant little volume."—*Yorkshire Post.*

"A little volume calculated to interest many an adult reader as well as gladden a child's heart. . . . We hope it will be widely circulated as a gift-book for the young."—*Bradford Chronicle.*

"Sixteen as nice little stories about fairy children, elfin sprites, talking flowers, whispering shells, and twittering birds, as any fanciful little lady or gentleman would care to read, all illustrated by a new artist who shows that she fully understands and appreciates the spirit of her author."—*Bookseller.*

"A very charming series of ' tales of fairy lore, truth twined in fancy's thread of light ' which we can confidently recommend as a most suitable gift to intelligent children of twelve and upwards. Juvenile readers once launched among these pleasant stories are not likely to lay the book down until it is read through."—*Midland Counties Herald.*

"A charming child's book. . . . It appeals to the more refined among the children. The tales are new and fantastic, full of strange conceits and original devices."—*Lloyd's Newspaper.*

HOULSTON AND SONS, 7, PATERNOSTER BUILDINGS.